Porsche 911 3.2 Carrera
The last of the evolution

Other great books from Veloce –

Essential Buyer's Guide Series
Porsche 911 (964) (Streather)
Porsche 911 (993) (Streather)
Porsche 911 (996) (Streather)
Porsche 911 Carrera 3.2 (Streather)
Porsche 911SC (Streather)
Porsche 924 (Hodgkins)
Porsche 928 (Hemmings)
Porsche 930 Turbo & 911 (930) Turbo (Streather)
Porsche 944 (Higgins & Mitchell)
Porsche 986 Boxster (Streather)
Porsche 987 Boxster & Cayman (Streather)
Porsche 987 Boxster & Cayman –2nd Generation (Streather)

General
Porsche 356 (2nd Edition) (Long)
Porsche 908 (Födisch, Neßhöver, Roßbach, Schwarz & Roßbach)
Porsche 911 Carrera – The Last of the Evolution (Corlett)
Porsche 911R, RS & RSR, 4th Edition (Starkey)
Porsche 911, The Book of the (Long)
Porsche 911 – The Definitive History 1963-1971 (Long)
Porsche 911 – The Definitive History 1971-1977 (Long)
Porsche 911 – The Definitive History 1977-1987 (Long)
Porsche 911 – The Definitive History 1987-1997 (Long)
Porsche 911 – The Definitive History 1997-2004 (Long)
Porsche 911SC 'Super Carrera' – The Essential Companion (Streather)
Porsche 914 & 914-6: The Definitive History of the Road & Competition Cars (Long)
Porsche 924 (Long)
Porsche 928 (Long)
Porsche 944 (Long)
Porsche 964, 993 & 996 Data Plate Code Breaker (Streather)
Porsche 993 'King Of Porsche' – The Essential Companion (Streather)
Porsche 996 'Supreme Porsche' – The Essential Companion (Streather)
Porsche 997 'Porsche Excellence' – The Essential Companion (Streather)
Porsche Boxster – The 986 Series 1996-2004 (Long)
Porsche Racing Cars – 1953 to 1975 (Long)
Porsche Racing Cars – 1976 to 2005 (Long)
Porsche - The Racing 914s (Smith)
Porsche – The Rally Story (Meredith)
Porsche: Three Generations of Genius (Meredith)

www.veloce.co.uk

First published in 2005, reprinted in 2007, January 2010 & May 2015. This edition published March 2017 by Veloce Publishing Limited, Veloce House, Parkway Farm Business Park, Poundbury, Dorchester, Dorset, DT1 3AR, England. Fax 01305 268864/e-mail info@veloce.co.uk/web www.veloce.co.uk or www.velocebooks.com.
ISBN: 978-1-787110-97-7 UPC: 6-36847-01097-3
© Tony Corlett and Veloce Publishing 2005, 2007, 2010, 2015 & 2017. All rights reserved. With the exception of quoting brief passages for the purpose of review, no part of this publication may be recorded, reproduced or transmitted by any means, including photocopying, without the written permission of Veloce Publishing Ltd. Throughout this book logos, model names and designations, etc, have been used for the purposes of identification, illustration and decoration. Such names are the property of the trademark holder as this is not an official publication.
Readers with ideas for automotive books, or books on other transport or related hobby subjects, are invited to write to the editorial director of Veloce Publishing at the above address.
British Library Cataloguing in Publication Data – A catalogue record for this book is available from the British Library. Typesetting, design and page make-up all by Veloce Publishing Ltd on Apple Mac. Printed and Bound by CPI Group (UK) Ltd, Croydon, CR04YY.

Porsche 911 3.2 Carrera
The last of the evolution

Tony Corlett

VELOCE PUBLISHING
THE PUBLISHER OF FINE AUTOMOTIVE BOOKS

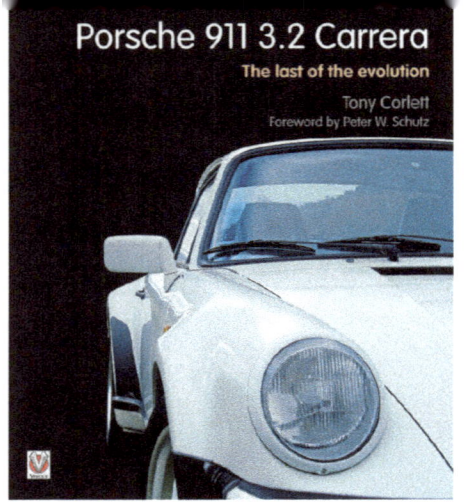

Contents

About the author 5
Foreword 6
Introduction 7

Chapter 1 911 the complete evolution 10

Chapter 2 History 12

Chapter 3 Model specifications 18
   Coupé 18
   Targa 19
   Cabriolet 20

Chapter 4 The Carrera - designed to drive 21

Chapter 5 M491 Turbo-look/Supersport
equipment: Wide body 28

Chapter 6 M637 Club sport: Blueprinted 36
   M637 chassis specification 36
   Engine 38
   Transmission 38
   Suspension, wheels, tyres 38
   Aerodynamics 38

Chapter 7 M503 911 Speedster: Bott's creation ... 45

Chapter 8 The engine - type 930 53

Chapter 9 Ignition and fuel injection 55
   Bosch Motronic ML 3.1 55

Chapter 10 Transmission - 915 to G50 56

Chapter 11 Suspension 58

Chapter 12 Fuchs felge 59

Chapter 13 Chassis numbers 61

Chapter 14 Factory prices 63

Chapter 15 Manufacture codes 65
   International 'C' codes 65
   Standard UK specification for 1987 (C16) 65
   Standard USA specification for 1987 66

Chapter 16 Colours 70

Chapter 17 Official factory Production
numbers 73

Chapter 18 Zuffenhausen - 1984 to 1989 75
   Research and development 76

Chapter 19 Exterior aesthetics 81

Chapter 20 Interior 89

Chapter 21 Attention to detail 96

Chapter 22 At the controls 100
   The standard layout of a 1984
   dashboard and controls as shown
   in the Porsche handbook: 103

Chapter 23 Driving impressions 104

Chapter 24 On the track 108
   In the dry 108
   In the wet 111

Chapter 25 953 4x4 Paris to Dakar 115

Chapter 26 CTR Yellow Bird 118
   Group C Turbo Ruf (CTR) 118

Chapter 27 Porsche vs Ferrari 124
   Carrera vs 328 124

Chapter 28 Improving excellence: Upgrading 131
   Engine 131
   Handling 133
   Brakes 134
   Wheels and tyres 135
   Interior 136

Chapter 29 Over the mountain 137

Chapter 30 Spirit of Carrera 141

Chapter 31 Technical overview 144

Chapter 32 Technical data 148

Index 159

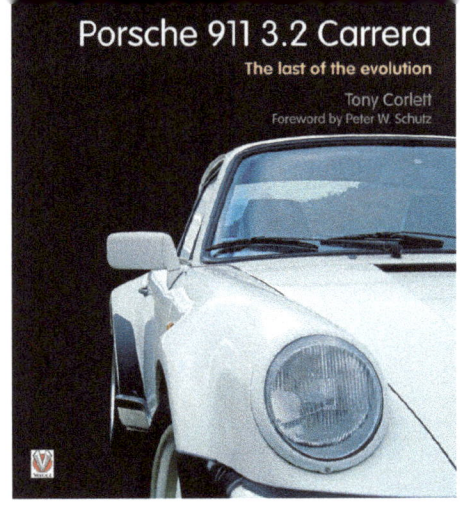

About the Author

Although I've been involved with sports cars for many years (including Ferraris, Alfa Romeos, Lotus, McLarens and Porsches), as time's gone by I've found myself becoming increasingly interested in the cars produced in the nineteen-eighties (the last of what I regard as the 'true grit' sports machines). Chief among these is the Porsche 911, and, in particular, the last of the 911 evolution, the 3.2 Carrera.

In the early 'eighties I was employed as a time keeper by Scuderia Ferrari, working alongside such greats as Gilles Villeneuve, Didier Pironi, Patrick Tambay and Rene Arnoux, as well as Mauro Forgheiri, the then Ferrari team boss. I returned to Ferrari as a project manager in the late eighties, and I headed the development of Ferrari's United Kingdom Formula One design facility, working directly as a consultant to John Barnard and Peter Reinhart.

After this period with Ferrari, I went to work for McLaren Cars as a consultant overseeing the development of the McLaren F1 road car production factory (reporting directly to Jeff Hazell, ex-team manager from Williams Grand Prix Engineering).

I've contributed articles and photographs for various publications, journals and books during the eighties and, in 1983, while performing a stint with Charles Ivey and the Group B Porsche 930 Turbo, I appeared in the video *In Car 962* with Derek Bell.

I've been the Register Secretary of the Porsche Club Great Britain, 911 3.2 Carrera, for four years now, and have amassed a great deal of information on, and photographs of, these great cars. This book, then, which is based on that experience, is a nostalgic wander back through the nineteen-eighties with one of the greatest cars ever built. I hope you enjoy reading it as much as I have enjoyed writing it.

Tony Corlett with his 1984 Carrera.

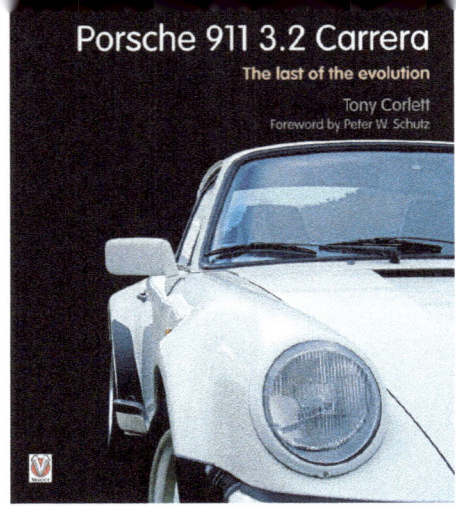

Foreword by Peter W. Schutz (CEO Porsche AG 1981-1987)

The Porsche 924, 944 and 928, the vehicles intended to replace the unorthodox 911, were like figure skaters with their arms extended for slow spins. The engine in the front and transmission in the rear were designed to optimise stability instead of manoeuvrability. This resulted in stable touring cars that were outstanding technical achievements, but not real Porsches in the eyes of the Porsche faithful.

None of these new vehicles was able to replace the about-to-be-discontinued Porsche 911 in the hearts of customers and dealers. It was essential for us to recognize what our faithful customers were looking for, and to make sure we gave it to them.

A deep sense of loss, a grieving that was almost heartbreaking, was gathering like a storm. The new Porsche offerings could not replace the revered 911. To me, a newcomer, the feeling of impending catastrophe was overpowering.

The decision to keep the 911 in the product line occurred one afternoon in the office of Dr Helmuth Bott, the Porsche operating board member responsible for all engineering and development. I noticed a chart on the wall of Professor Bott's office. It depicted the ongoing development schedules for the three primary Porsche product lines: 944, 928 and 911. Two of them stretched far into the future, but the 911 program stopped at the end of 1981. I remember rising from my chair, walking over to the chart, taking a black marker pen, and extending the 911 program bar clean off the end of the chart. I am sure I heard a silent cheer from Professor Bott, and I knew I had done the right thing. The Porsche 911, the company icon, had been saved, and I believe the company was saved with it.

Peter W Schutz, CEO of Porsche AG, 1981 to 1987, with a 911 Carrera.

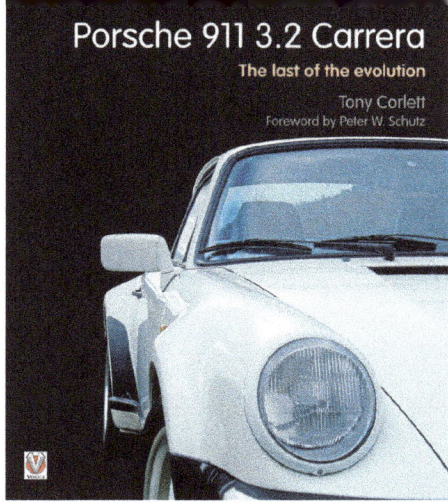

Introduction

"Driving in its purest form," is how the sales brochure describes the 3.2 Carrera. With regard to the engine performance, it goes on to say, "The advanced specification has resulted in the 3.2-litre engine of the 911 Carrera model developing 231bhp (DIN) at 5900rpm with a 10.3:1 compression ratio. The 3164cc engine's maximum torque of 284Nm at 4800rpm indicates its excellent flexibility, enabling 0-62.5mph acceleration in 6.1 seconds and a maximum speed of 152mph, regardless of body style".

When considering that the 3.2 Carrera has none of the later electronic aids, nor any special safety features like ABS or power steering, perhaps the sales brochure is right, and it is indeed driving in its purest form.

The confidence you feel in a well set up Carrera is something quite special. While there is a tendency towards mild understeer in harder cornering situations, generally the car feels as if it's on rails. It turns in with sharp precision and, once through the apex of the curve, the power can be applied quite harshly.

Savour the sound of the (glorious) flat six engine and watch the needle, in the massive centrally-mounted rev counter, climb round into the red. Power delivery is smooth, and then at a little over 4000rpm the engine note changes and it digs a little deeper right up to the red line. Speeds in excess of 120mph can be achieved without really trying. Road conditions and safety considerations allowing, you'll feel at one with the progressive power and the overall tautness of the chassis. Once you've taken a 911 Carrera to the limit, you'll want to turn around and do it all again.

Although the steering is heavy, the chassis hard, and the gear change demanding, driving a 911 is a memorable experience - the feeling of man and machine in complete harmony.

Model versions
• Carrera: Standard Body with Teledial cast alloy wheels.
• Sport Equipment (SE) / Carrera Sport Package: As standard but with front and rear aerodynamic spoilers, sport shock absorbers and wider road wheels (lightweight cast or forged) with low profile tyres.
• Turbo-Look (TL) or Supersport Equipment (SSE): As standard, but with the wider Turbo body, front and rear aerodynamic spoilers as fitted to the Turbo, an ultra-high performance braking system, uprated suspension and shock absorbers, wider lightweight forged road wheels with ultra-low profile tyres.
• Club Sport (CS): A lighter and simplified variant of the Sport-equipped Coupé.
• Speedster: A lowered variant of the Cabriolet with Turbo-Look optional body.
• Silver Anniversary and Celebration models celebrating 25 years of the 911 and the 250,000th 911.

Body types
Coupé: All steel roof incorporating a sun-roof as an option.
Targa: Removable full-width roof panel and wraparound rear screen.

Factory photograph of the 911 Carrera Coupé.

Cabriolet: Electrically operated folding Mohair soft-top roof.

PRODUCTION YEARS
1984 - E Program
1985 - F Program
1986 - G Program
1987 - H Program
1988 - J Program
1989 - K Program

UPGRADES
1987 (H Program) replaced Porsche 915 gearbox with Getrag G50, the latter having a shorter shift and hydraulic clutch operation.

OPTIONS
Many options were offered, varying from car to car. Option codes for each chassis number are listed in the car's original handbook and on a sticker under the bonnet lid. The option codes are also available from Porsche (as related to specific chassis numbers).

ACKNOWLEDGEMENTS
This book was written with the assistance and support of Dr Ing hc F Porsche (Porsche AG) in Stuttgart, for which I am extremely grateful. I am particularly indebted to Klaus Parr (Archive), Tilman Brodbeck (Excellence), Annemarie Reinhardt (Legal).

Special thanks goes to Peter W Schutz, ex-Porsche AG Chairman/CEO, who not only wrote the foreword for this book, but also offered me inside knowledge into the exact moment the 911 was saved from discontinuation. After six World Sports Car Championships, three Formula One World Championships, and seven profitable years, Peter retired from Porsche at the end of 1987.

Thanks to Otto Fuchs KG, Bosch, Getrag, RUF, and the Porsche Club Great Britain.

Amongst the many individual enthusiasts who contributed to this book, my sincere thanks goes to:
Paul Dangerfield: Technical and background assistance, technical checking.
Paul Cadrobbi: USA Turbo-Look assistance.
Michael Chadwick: Club Sport assistance.
Steve Darnell: Club Sport assistance.
Chris Davenport: Speedster assistance.
Richard Bernau: Upgrade assistance.
Jorg Ludwig: Fuchs assistance.
Alois Ruf and Marc Bonger: RUF assistance.

I am very grateful to the many owners and photographers whose cars

Factory photograph of the 911 Carrera Coupé with 'Turbo-Look' option.

and photographs appear in the book: Jamie Brundell, Mike Chadwick, Mark Clair, Alan Cordery, (Tony Corlett), Steve Darnell, Chris Davenport, Darren Fink, John Gaisford, Island Photographics, Brice Kadel, Masaru Kagami, Lloyd Langley, Jonathan Madden, Bernie Magee, Gordon McKay, Steve Miller, Paul Narcisse Jr, Kevin Post, Peter Robain, Dale Smith, Andy Tims, Tom Trudell, Steve Upsdell, Salvador Valiente, William Vogl and Bill Waite.

Cover shot: Bernie Magee's Grand Prix White Supersport - photographer: Tony Corlett.

For general assistance: Geoff Ives, Bernie Magee, Mario Lusardi, Gordon McKay, Julian Trinder and Steve Upsdell.

I am indebted to all the other Carrera owners around the world with whom I have communicated over the years, all of whom share the same passion.

The 'Carrera' script, reproduction of the driver's handbook, official Carrera promotional photographs, 1964 911 promotional photograph, and 1984 Paris to Dakar poster are all (officially) used with the kind permission of Porsche AG The 1984 Paris to Dakar screen captures were reproduced by and used with kind permission from Duke International Limited.

Tony Corlett, Isle of Man

Handbook cover.

911 Carrera

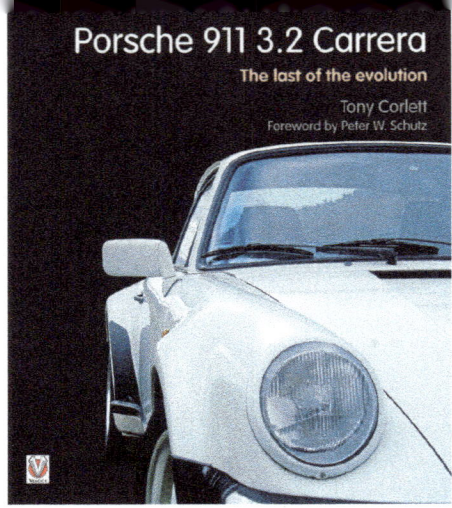

Chapter 1

911 The complete evolution

1963
Model 901 launched on 12th September 1963 at the Frankfurt Show.

1964
'O' Series
Model 911 goes into production - type number changed from 901 to 911.
911 2.0: 130bhp
Engine capacity is 1991cc
Price DM 21,900

1965
911 2.0: 130bhp
Targa model introduced

1966
911 2.0: 130bhp
100,000th 911 rolls off the production line

1967
911 2.0: 130bhp
911S: 160bhp
Forged alloy wheel rims (Fuchs) introduced

1968
'A' Series
911 T: 110bhp - replaced 912
911 L: 130bhp
911 S: 160bhp
Sportomatic gearbox introduced

1969
'B' Series
911 T: 110bhp
911 E: 130bhp
911 S: 160bhp
Wheelbase increased on all 911 models from 2211mm to 2268mm

1970
'C' Series
Engine capacity increases to 2195cc

1971
'D' Series
911 T: 125bhp
911 E: 155bhp
911 S: 180bhp

1972
'E' Series
Engine capacity (Capacity) increases to 2341cc
911 T: 130bhp
911 E: 165bhp
911 S: 190bhp
915 4-speed gearbox introduced

1973
'F' Series
911 T: 130bhp
911 E: 165bhp
911 S: 190bhp
911 RS Carrera 2.7: 210bhp
Wheelbase increased on all 911 models from 2268mm to 2272mm
Carrera name used for the first time
Rear 'ducktail' spoiler introduced

1974
'G' Series
Engine capacity increases to 2687cc
911 2.7: 150bhp
911 2.7 S: 175bhp
Impact bumpers introduced

1975
'H' Series
911 2.7: 150bhp
911 2.7 S: 175bhp
911 Turbo 3.0: 260bhp

911 Carrera

The first production sports car to have an exhaust-driven turbocharger
Long-term corrosion protection introduces galvanised zinc coating

1976
'I' Series
Engine capacity increased to 2994cc
911 2.7: 150bhp
911 2.7 S: 175bhp
911 Carrera 3.0: 200bhp
911 Turbo 3.0: 260bhp

1977
'K' Series
911 2.7: 150bhp
911 2.7 S: 175bhp
911 Carrera 3.0: 200bhp
911 Turbo 3.0: 260bhp
250,000th Porsche rolls off the production line - 911 2.7

1978
'L' Series
911 SC: 180bhp
911 Turbo 3.3: 300bhp
Bosch 'K' Jetronic Injection
11 blade fan
Cast alloy wheels optional

1979
911 SC: 180bhp
911 Turbo 3.3: 300bhp
Catalytic converter introduced to 911 range

1980
'A' Programme
911 SC: 180bhp
911 Turbo 3.3: 300bhp
915 5-speed gearbox introduced

1981
'B' Programme
911 SC: 204bhp
911 Turbo 3.3: 300bhp

1982
'C' Programme
911 SC: 204bhp
911 Turbo 3.3: 300bhp
911 SC Cabriolet
The first 911 Cabriolet

1983
'D' Programme
911 SC: 204bhp
911 Turbo 3.3: 300bhp

1984
'E' Programme
Engine capacity increases to 3164cc
911 3.2 Carrera: 231bhp
911 Turbo 3.3: 300bhp
911 4x4 wins the Paris to Dakar rally
Turbo or wide body option included - known as Turbo-Look (TL) and Supersport Equipment (SSE)

1985
'F' Programme
911 3.2 Carrera: 231bhp
911 Turbo 3.3: 300bhp

1986
'G' Programme
911 3.2 Carrera: 231bhp
911 Turbo 3.3: 300bhp

1987
'H' Programme
911 3.2 Carrera: 231bhp
911 Carrera Club Sport: 231bhp

911 Turbo 3.3: 300bhp
G50 gearbox introduced

1988
'J' Programme
911 3.2 Carrera: 231bhp
911 Carrera Club Sport: 231bhp
911 Turbo 3.3: 300bhp

1989
'K' Programme
911 3.2 Carrera: 231bhp
911 Carrera Club Sport: 231bhp
911 3.2 Speedster: 231bhp
911 Turbo 3.3: 300bhp

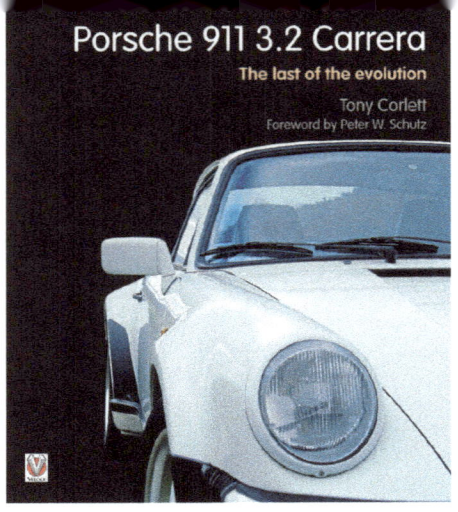

Chapter 2

History

From its inception in 1963, the Porsche 911, which went from strength to strength under the control of Fritz Bezner and Bernd Kahnau, was the subject of one of the longest periods of continuous development of any car. However, although there were development drawings and specifications, no-one really ever 'designed' a new 911, which is why the basic concept remained throughout its evolution. Each evolution really only meant a bigger engine and more power.

Handling, comfort and accessories were improved, but the established formula remained (indeed, the body design was considered to be beyond improvement, only requiring cosmetic changes to keep it up to date).

By 1984, though, when the 911 was 21, the design was regarded as being rather dated and old fashioned, and the intention was for it to be discontinued. It was pure chance that secured the continuation of the 911 and thus the creation of the 3.2 Carrera.

The distinctive rear aerodynamic spoiler was fitted to the Sport equipped Carrera. Reshaped for the Carrera in 1984, this gave the then new 911 a fresh visual identity compared to its predecessor the 911 SC. This rear tail was designed to be aerodynamically smoother and less of a dirt trap.

1984 Carrera Coupé with Sport Equipment.

Claimed to be substantially new, the 3.2-litre Carrera was hailed as an altogether improved car over its predecessor, the 3-litre SC. The biggest change was the engine, 80 per cent of which Porsche claimed was new. Still using the 95mm bore of the SC, it now incorporated the stroke of the 930 Turbo, increasing the capacity to 3164cc and lifting the power to 231bhp. Marrying this engine to the Bosch Motronic DME (Digital Motor Electronics) controlled fuel injection system allowed the compression ratio to be raised from 9.8:1 to 10.3:1. It also created a very fuel-efficient unit, improving power output, torque, pollution levels, and cold start operation. To eliminate the ongoing problem with the 911 engine chain tensioners, the Carrera chain tensioners became hydraulically-operated. The cylinder designed to keep the chain under tension was now fed directly by an engine oil pressure circuit.

The braking system was also improved. The front and rear discs were increased by 4mm to 24mm thick, and the rear calliper pistons were increased to 42mm diameter. A pressure regulator was included in the rear brake circuit.

The basic bodywork, suspension configuration, and most of the interior were copied from the SC, but the Carrera was more luxurious. Other differences included a rear engine lid 'Carrera' logo, integrated front fog lights, a more streamlined rear wing, a new ventilation system, new seats, and various interior modifications.

During its six years of production, the biggest improvement came in 1987 with the introduction of the newly-designed type G50 gearbox, manufactured by Getrag. This replaced the old and generally more bulky Porsche-built type 915 gearbox. The new G50 used Borg-Warner synchronisers and provided an improved gear change and shortened shift distance. At the same time, an hydraulically-operated clutch was introduced to replace the original cable-operated system. The diameter of

Carrera Club Sport.

Carrera Cabriolet 1984 to 1989.

Carrera Speedster 1989.

Carrera Turbo-Look 1984 to 1989.

1984 to 1986 rear light cluster with under-bumper fog lights for European cars and full width Porsche script logo.

India Red Carrera Coupé: Sport Equipment, with front and rear aerodynamic spoilers and Fuchs alloy wheels. The car is fitted with 16in diameter wheels finished in standard black paint.

The Carrera Cabriolet was the brainchild of the then new Porsche chairman Peter W Schutz.

the clutch was increased from 225mm to 240mm. The incorporation of this new gearbox also brought about rear floorpan and torsion bar modifications.

The Carrera was also available with the Turbo-Look option, which used the standard Carrera power plant and drivetrain, but featured larger brake callipers and turbo-style rear trailing arms.

For 1987 and 1988, and in limited numbers for 1989, the Carrera Club Sport was introduced. This was a limited production run, lightweight option, weighing 50kg less than the standard sport-equipped Coupé. Ready for racing, the Club Sport was stripped of fog lights, air-conditioning, power seats, rear seats, undercoating and sound deadening, but included stiffer Bilstein Special dampers, sports seats, hollow stem valves, and a re-programmed ECU chip.

In 1988 and 1989, to celebrate both the 25th year since the original 901 presentation and the production of the 250,000th 911, Porsche produced special edition models know as 'Silver Anniversary' and 'Celebration' models. The latter Celebration model for 1988 was not too different from the standard Sport-equipped Coupé, this Carrera came in (special) Diamond Blue Metallic paint, colour-coded wheels, and a Silver Blue leather interior. It also had an imprint of Ferry Porsche's signature on the headrests, in recognition of his ongoing involvement with the 911.

In 1989, the Carrera Speedster was introduced. This design succeeded in capturing the character of previous and historic Porsche Speedsters. With an even lower windscreen, 'speedster humps' and soft top roof, it was a combination of Club Sport and Cabriolet. Unlike the Club Sport, however, the Speedster also came with a popular wide body option.

In 1989 the 3.2 Carrera was discontinued and the evolution based on the original 911 ended with it. It made way for the newer technology and aerodynamic sophistication of the new 964 (designated 911 for marketing purposes only, which means that the 3.2 Carrera was the last Porsche to carry the 911 brand as a factory designated

Chapter 3

Model specifications

Coupé

Chassis code 10 or 12. The Coupé was, of course, the original 901 design from the pen of Alexander 'Butzi' Porsche. Apart from some minor changes, the shape of the Coupé remained the same from its inception in 1963 to the last of the 3.2 Carreras in 1989.

The term coupé describes a two-door car with a sweeping rear screen. The 'C' posts usually incorporate a set of rear seats and a luggage compartment. Porsche chose to use the luggage compartment to house the engine, but the basic sloping design was maintained. Unbelievably, no other motor manufacturer has successfully copied the 911 Coupé shape, which leaves this masterpiece with a monopoly in an otherwise copy-cat world. Very much drawn from the original Volkswagen Beetle and the later Porsche 356 shapes, the 911 Coupé shape is iconic and unmistakable.

USA specification Coupé, Targa and Cabriolet.

Factory promotional photograph of a 1987 Sport equipped Coupé.

Factory promotional photograph of a 1984 Targa.

TARGA

Chassis code 14 or 16. Introduced in 1965, the Targa was Porsche's response to the demand for open-top motoring from customers who favoured the 356 cabriolets. Faced with two major problems (the cost of tooling up for a new car, and a lack of body rigidity once the roof was removed from the Coupé) Porsche retained as many of the Coupé body panels as possible, and incorporated a stainless steel roll-over bar. All the panels below the waist line remained the same, thus saving tooling costs, although the incorporation of the roll-over bar required some minor reinforcements in the floorpan. This produced an acceptably rigid open-top car without a major weight gain.

The Targa, with its removable lateral panel between the top of the windscreen and the 'B' post roll-over bar (or, as it's more commonly known, the 'Targa Bar') was a popular Carrera option. In order to incorporate the Targa Bar into the Coupé shape, Porsche chose to increase the size of the rear screen. Originally a zip out plastic screen, this was later changed to glass and wrapped around to the 'B' posts, thereby eliminating the 'C' post altogether. This gave a more airy feel to the cabin and, once the Targa roof was removed, an almost total cabriolet feel could be achieved.

19

Factory promotional photograph of a 1984 Cabriolet.

Cabriolet

Chassis code 15 or 17. The brainchild of Peter Schutz and engineered by an original 356 Cabriolet engineer, Herr Bauer, the 911 Cabriolet was born from the carcass of a 911 Targa. First shown in 1981 at Frankfurt, interestingly as a four-wheel drive Turbo, the Cabriolet entered production in 1982.

Bauer almost achieved perfection with soft-top design in the 911 Cabriolet. This was a 911 with a soft-top that maintained a lot of the classic Coupé lines. Leaving the Coupé windscreen and 'A' posts in place, the Carrera Cabriolet looked as good with the roof up as it did with it folded down. In order to maintain the stiffness of the chassis, Porsche incorporated reinforcements within the lower chassis sills, thus eliminating much of the chassis twist associated with roof removal. Scuttle-shake and chassis-sag were thus avoided, and the doors on the Cabriolet operated as perfectly as they did on the Coupé.

In 1985, Porsche showed a Turbo-Look Cabriolet with an aluminium detachable hardtop at the Swedish Motor Show. The style of this was such that, at a glance, it could easily be mistaken for a Coupé. Referred to in the Porsche literature from 1986, a galvanised steel hardtop was made available.

One further addition made to the Cabriolet was an engine vibration damper. This was a strut that sat to the rear left of the engine and was designed to eliminate engine vibration through the chassis.

Since Targa and Cabriolet production was carried out in conjunction with the Coupé, Porsche was able to maximise its manufacturing process in one sequence.

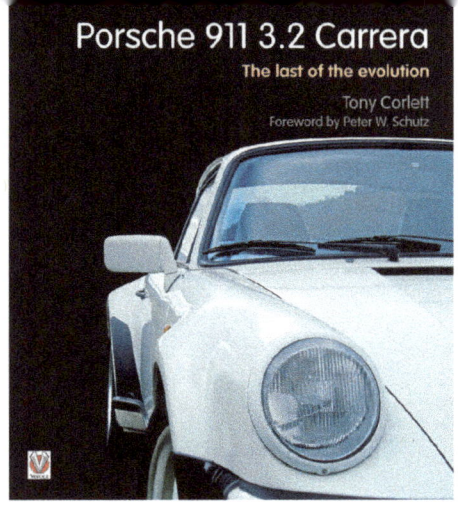

CHAPTER 4

THE CARRERA - DESIGNED TO DRIVE

Because the basic 911 shape remained much the same from 1963 through to 1989, it is understandable that Porsche chose to keep the 911 factory designation during this period. The rear engine configuration was not new in 1963, of course, as both Porsche and Volkswagen used the Ferdinand Porsche layout to great effect in the Porsche 356 and VW Beetle. The 911, however, or 901 as it was originally named, was an attempt to achieve the optimum form in a configuration no other manufacturer was even contemplating. The 356, albeit a great little car, was never going to be a supercar, but with the 911, Porsche has never really looked back.

Following on from the 911 SC, the 3.2 Carrera brought even better performance and roadholding to the 911 evolution, whilst maintaining the essence of a practical 2+2 sports car. The heart of the new 911 was a 3.2 litre, flat-six air-cooled engine which remained faithful to the original engine concept. With consistent development, the engine was one of the most efficient, economical, and environmentally acceptable performance engines available. Capable of stunning performance, this engine also returned fuel economy never before seen in a performance car. The flat-six configuration was always exceptionally smooth, and the 3.2-litre version was no exception.

Unconventional, perhaps, but respected, definitely. The 3.2 flat-six was compact and relatively light, due to the lightweight silicon aluminium alloy engine block and light alloy cylinders and cylinder heads. With superbly balanced crankshaft (forged steel) and connecting rods, achieved using twelve counterweights with eight main bearings, the 3164cc (cubic centimetre) engine was exceptionally smooth. With two valves per cylinder in a 'V' configuration, the intake and exhaust valves were positioned perfectly to ensure maximum flow of inlet and exhaust gases. The double overhead camshafts, oil scavenger and pressure pumps were chain driven. The chain was kept at the correct tension by way of force-feed lubrication and self-adjusting, maintenance free chain tensioners (a vast improvement over earlier 911 engines).

The 3.2 Carrera had a 42 per cent to 58 per cent weight distribution, front to rear, the 911 Turbo narrowly beating it at 38 per cent to 62 per cent. With nearly 60 per cent loading over the rear driving wheels, due mainly to the rear-mounted engine, the Carrera had almost unequalled power transfer to the road. It delivered power without any appreciable loss of grip, ensuring good overall traction on all road surfaces.

The engine was cooled by a distinctive, centrally-mounted, direct-

The 911 rear wheelarches are legendary, blending with the wings and flanks in perfect harmony.

The standard Carrera Coupé came without the aerodynamic front and rear spoilers. The rear engine cover incorporated a slatted grille where the spoiler would be fitted. The fan sucks the air through this grille and onto the engine.

drive axial flow fan which produced a massive 1500 litres of air per second at 6000rpm across the entire engine surface. Air was sucked in through the grill in the top of the engine cover by the fan located behind the engine. In front of the fan was a shroud that directed the air over the crankcase and cylinder barrels. Deflector panels were fitted around each barrel to ensure even cooling. These deflectors directed the air downwards and across the exhaust to aid exhaust cooling. The air was then deflected downwards and away from the engine towards the road surface.

The air cooling was complemented by a dry-sump oil lubrication system. The mass of the engine oil was stored in a remote oil reservoir, a design feature taken directly from motor racing success, which ensured a continuous oil supply even under severe lateral cornering. The oil was cooled twice, once through a crankcase-mounted oil cooler located within the 'fan' air-flow, and secondly, via a front-mounted oil cooler located under the right front wing. The oil circulated from the engine via the oil cooler radiators and was delivered back to the reservoir. In all 911 engines, the oil assisted in maintaining engine temperature, and it was essential that the oil was of a sufficiently high quality.

The gearbox was mounted directly to the front of the engine. Power was delivered through the flywheel and single dry-plate clutch combination, and transmitted to the drive wheels via articulated halfshafts.

Fully independent, the Carrera suspension remained faithful to the original 901 design, offering precise handling and comfort in unison with the power output. From the start, bushing was kept to an absolute minimum. A very rigid body and chassis monocoque design, married to an uncompromising suspension layout, ensured that body roll was kept to a minimum during cornering. This ensured that the tyres had maximum adhesion under adverse lateral conditions.

Porsche expected that, in most cases, a normal 911 driver would only utilise about 40 to 50 per cent of the Carrera's cornering abilities. On a 190 meter radius track, the 3.2 Carrera achieved 85 per cent gravitational acceleration, in other words 0.85g, meaning that the Carrera would reach its cornering limits very late. The average limit for other competitive marques was stated as 0.76g, indicating that the Carrera outperformed most of its rivals.

Precise and responsive steering was achieved using a traditional rack and pinion system. The steering rack formed part of the track-rod and was self correcting, with no play whatsoever from lock to lock. Driver contact with the front wheels and the road was perfect, with every movement transferred directly through the steering wheel. This gave the driver a complete 'feel' for the car's road behaviour.

Stopping power was provided by a race-proven, servo-assisted, hydraulic dual circuit braking system with ventilated discs all round. The standard Carrera had cast-iron, two-piston brake callipers, while the Supersport version had aluminium four-piston brake callipers, all located so as to get maximum air-flow for cooling. The callipers were also positioned on the hub to minimise rotation forces from the wheels. The servo-assistance ensured maximum braking performance from minimal brake pedal pressure. The handbrake operated on the rear wheels only, via a

The duck tail was first introduced on the 911 2.7 RS in 1973, increased in size with the introduction of the Turbo in 1975, further increased in size to cope with the Turbo intercooler in 1978, and streamlined for the Carrera in 1984.

The 911 impact bumpers first made an appearance in 1974, and were carried through to the end of Carrera production in 1989. The front and rear aerodynamic spoilers greatly reduce lift, and provide much improved straight line stability. The aerodynamic effect was such that the chin spoiler was not fitted to Carreras without the rear spoiler, and vice versa.

separate drum inside the disc housing. This ensured that any excessive heat built up in the discs could still dissipate when the handbrake was applied, thus avoiding problems of disk warping.

As for aerodynamics, Porsche claimed a drag coefficient of Cd 0.39 and a frontal area, for the standard car, of 1.77 square meters.

The body and overall appearance of the 911 Carrera was something to behold. Unsurpassed finish quality and fitment ensured the 911 experience began long before its performance was appreciated. A single piece monocoque shell, incorporating the body, floor pan and chassis components, was completely hot-dip galvanized (a quenching process which applied a rust-inhibiting zinc coating to the steel). The front wings, doors, boot lid and engine cover, also hot-dip galvanised, completed the full body. The main flanks, rear wings and roof formed part of the single piece body shell.

To front and rear were wraparound aluminium bumpers, painted to match the body colour. They were made from 5-6 millimetre thick aluminium sheet and were mounted remotely to the main body. This provided a slip-plane in which they were able to move laterally to the body in case of crash impact. These 'impact-bumpers', first introduced to the 911 in 1974 to suit American safety legislation, were mounted on shock-absorbing dampers and designed to operate when bumped at low speed. Following stringent testing under both low and high speed conditions, the results showed that at low speed, no damage at all was done to the body, while at high speed, damage was kept to a minimum.

The most important aspect of this safety technology was the front crumple zone, which absorbed energy in the case of a frontal crash. The bonnet was designed to deform in a predetermined way, and the firm hinge mountings prevented the bonnet intruding into the passenger cabin. Because the impact resistant fuel cell was mounted at the front, it incorporated a closed evaporation system and protected pipes to prevent fuel escaping in roll-over crashes. Attention was also paid to the layout of the front radius arms, or lower wishbones, which provided protection to the cell.

The safety cell of the Carrera was extremely strong, and would withstand impact from front or side. The side doors were fitted with 'safety-locks', designed to keep them closed and in position during impact. In a 30mph frontal impact, the safety cell performed well enough to ensure that the doors could be opened after the incident and that the seat belt fixing points did not fail.

The integral roof and strong side pillars provided exceptional roll-over protection. In crash test simulations, the Carrera was catapulted sideways at 30mph and repeatedly rolled over, simulating a critical crash condition. The results showed that the entire safety cell performed admirably. Both doors remained firmly shut, ensuring integrity of the safety cell, and opened freely afterwards.

The interior of the Carrera was just as safe, with energy absorbing material incorporated at all critical points. All the instrument panel switches and the glove compartment lock, for example, were made from deformable materials. The rear view mirror was mounted on a deformable stalk, and all materials used were flame retardant. Inertia reel seat belts and safety glass all round completed the internal safety features. Outside the car, foldable rubber-edged mirrors and rubber body extremities ensured pedestrian injury was kept to a minimum.

At the front, external lighting was by way of large, H4 halogen headlamps, two valance-mounted driving lamps and two bumper-mounted indicators. The rear had a lateral lighting cluster incorporating brake lights, indicators

Exacting body panel fit.

and reversing lamps. On the early Carreras, a high density rear fog lamp was positioned under the rear bumper, whereas on the later Carreras two fog lamps were incorporated into the lighting and reflector cluster. The Porsche script logo across the rear of the lighting cluster was also reduced in width on later cars to allow the fog lamps to be fitted.

The Carrera body shape was classic 911, the pure lines of which were only interrupted three times during its history. The first time was in 1973 with the addition of the rear 'duck-tail'; the second time was when the bumpers were changed in 1974; and the third time was when the body was widened for the turbo in 1975. Although the aerodynamic additions of rear wing and chin spoilers developed through various stages of design and development, the overall shape remained the same.

Amongst the many options, the Carrera was available with the more modern rear wing and chin spoiler for the Sport Equipment cars. The rear wing was redesigned to be more streamlined than that of the Turbo or SC. Shaped for smoother air-flow and to prevent the build up of dirt, this resulted in sleeker and lower side up-stands. This feature set the Carrera apart from the SC at a glance, the latter sporting the full turbo wing. However, the Carrera Supersport, bred from its turbo sister, did carry the full turbo rear wing.

Wind tunnel testing showed that the Carrera's chin spoiler and rear wing greatly reduced lift at high speeds. Porsche claimed that the front chin spoiler reduced underbody turbulence and that the large rear spoiler enhanced the Carrera's straight-line running performance in reducing wind resistance, increasing stability, and reducing lift at high speed. These wind tunnel-developed aerodynamic aids, when fitted to the Carrera, reduced overall drag by 2 per cent, and reduced

The pure lines of the 911 remained largely unchanged from its introduction in 1963. Only three major changes were made throughout its life: the rear ducktail in 1973; the impact bumpers in 1974; and the wide body of the Turbo in 1975.

lift from 180kg at 150mph to just 17kg. Extensive wind tunnel testing also improved engine cooling and the position of passenger compartment ventilation inlets, as well as optimising noise reduction for the rubber door and window seals, mirrors and windscreen wipers.

The front and rear aerodynamic aids were designed to work together. Where the Carrera was marketed without the rear wing, Porsche found that the chin spoiler had to be removed because the pitching moment at high speeds would have upset the balance, causing serious oversteer. Also, it's worth noting that a Carrera could not be ordered without a chin spoiler if the rear wing was fitted, because the understeer would have been too great.

The 911 3.2 Carrera was marketed throughout the world in different formats and with a variety of options. In its basic form, the standard Carrera - or 'non-sport' as it became affectionately known - was a 'pure' 911 shape without the additional aerodynamic features of the Sport Equipment cars. The Sport Equipment option included the chin and rear spoilers, sport shock absorbers, and wider road wheels with low profile tyres. The Supersport Equipment option included extended or wide wheelarches front and rear, with front and rear aerodynamic spoilers as fitted to the Turbo. Also included was an ultra-high performance braking system, uprated suspension and shock absorbers, wider road wheels and low profile tyres.

In identifying the Carrera, Porsche chose to be discrete. The standard Porsche Stuttgart Shield took pride of place on the very front of the bonnet, as is the case with all 911 Porsches, and there was a 'Porsche' script logo across the rear light cluster and a delicate 'Carrera' script logo on the rear engine cover. Although bearing the name 'Carrera', chosen after racing successes in the Mexican 'La Carrera Panamericana' road race, only the Club Sport model carried the 'Carrera' script on the lower flanks and doors.

Although Porsche offered many optional extras, none of these detracted from the beauty of the Carrera - rather, in many ways, they served to enhance the already evolved car. Whether it was a limited slip differential or cruise control, leather trim or air conditioning, the Carrera could be made into an executive express with all the trappings of luxury, sophistication and comfort.

Traditionally entirely hand-built, the 3.2 Carrera also benefited from a largely hand-assembled engine. The end result was a car of such quality that Porsche was able to offer extensive mechanical and body warranties (a ten year anti-corrosion body warranty, and a two year or twelve thousand mile mechanical warranty).

The Carrera specification catered for all tastes. The purists could opt for the standard model, whereas the more sport inclined could opt for the Sport Equipment or Supersport Equipment. Regardless of which you chose, the basic 911 shape was recognisable and brought with it a sense of defying the establishment.

www.velocebooks.com / www.veloce.co.uk
Details of all current books • New book news • Special offers

United Kingdom C16 specification India Red Sport equipped Coupe. India Red was only used from 1984 to 1986 (changed to Indian Red from 1987). Although many believe otherwise, Porsche never produced the Carrera in Guards Red.

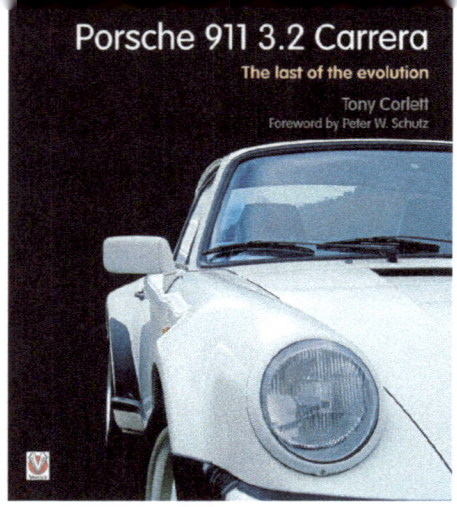

Chapter 5

M491 Turbo-Look/ Supersport Equipment: wide body

Although the Turbo-Look was born from the Carrera in 1984, investigation into early Turbo-Look documentation shows that some of the early cars didn't actually carry the 491 option code at all. This is a bit of a mystery, as the 1984 Carrera price reports: "*Turbo-Look (Karosserie, Fahrwerk, Bremsanlage wie 911 Turbo)*", and the 1984 Carrera handbook states: "*Fur den 911 Carrera mit Turbo-Look gelten, wenn nicht gesondert aufgefuhrt, die Angaben des 911 Carrera*". In other words, the Turbo-Look was definitely a recognized option from that date as a factory produced wide body. Exactly why option 491 was not previously stated still remains unclear. For this reason, the birth of the Turbo-Look, later known as 'Supersport Equipment' in Europe, is somewhat open to speculation.

While it's possible to determine the overall Carrera production numbers from official computer records at Porsche AG, including body types and international variants, the Turbo-Look was never specifically listed in Porsche production figures. Because of the apparent ambiguity surrounding the early European factory M491 Carreras, not even the option code listings can be relied upon. Since the chassis numbers for all Carreras do not differentiate options, the earlier Turbo-Look is not specifically denoted or easily spotted on paper. This problem is almost non-existent in America, however, as Porsche Cars North America did make a sustained effort to keep relatively accurate records of imports.

Unlike the Club Sport and Speedster, the latter also having the M491 option, the Turbo-Look or European Supersport did not get an official chassis recognition. This now legendary production code was not

Both pages: The Carrera Turbo-Look option was introduced by Porsche in 1984 to combat unofficial wide body copies built by independent coachbuilders. The M491 option code was used to denote the Turbo-Look. This is a later UK specification Supersport Coupé with the G50 gearbox.

This 1984 Turbo-Look in Platinum is thought to be the first imported into the USA. The American Turbo-Look came without the Carrera script on the engine cover. Only 421 Turbo-Look Coupés were imported into America in 1984.

The Turbo-Look or Supersport Equipment option for the Carrera used the wide body, suspension, wheels and brakes from the Turbo 911.

just a simple option number, unlike most of the other option codes that often represented only a single factor or accessory. Option M491 covered quite a bit more. Put simply, this was not just a wide body placed on a standard car.

As well as the rear suspension modifications and the wide front and rear wheelarches, the Turbo-Look also incorporated a Turbo rear spoiler, a wraparound Turbo chin spoiler, and Turbo wheels. Brake technology, derived from the 917 racing program, featured 285mm diameter cross-drilled discs to the front, and 290mm diameter cross-drilled discs to the rear, both with four-piston aluminium callipers. 1984 and 1985 Turbo-Look Carreras had 7x16 rims at the front and 8x16 rims at the rear, with the rears upsized to 9x16 from 1986 onwards, as was the case with the 911 Turbo.

The M491 option code was first used in the fabrication of the legendary 1973 RSR 2.8. Ingenious relocation of suspension pick-up points and modified trailing arms and wheel bearings allowed the cars to accommodate much wider wheels and tyres, keeping them firmly planted on the road. This option, created by Porsche engineers, was used on various wide-body competition 911s which remained at the cutting edge of international motorsport for a decade. Most notable were the 2.8 RSR and RS 3.0. Interestingly, from their inception in 1974, the iconic 911 Turbo Carreras were produced by installing a turbo engine and a stronger 4-speed gearbox into M491 optioned Carreras.

As the early 1975 911 Turbo Carrera quickly became an international sensation, many private coachbuilders recognized a niche market for transforming standard-bodied 911s into wide-bodied, Turbo-Looking cars. Porsche, not wanting to lose out, responded by returning to the pre-turbo production M491 optioned Carrera, and officially introducing it to the product range in 1984. Porsche's timing was in direct response to losing revenue due to independent tuners cashing in on Turbo Look 'knock-offs'. This was also Porsche's answer to a temporary withdrawal of the 911 Turbo from its largest market, North America. From 1980 onwards, more restrictive emissions controls in America saw the end of the 911 Turbo until 1986. Porsche had a growing void to fill. Many customers were left desperately wanting what they couldn't have, a fact which is backed-up by the American Turbo-Look sales figures for 1984 and 1985 of 423 and 391 respectively. When the 911 Turbo was reintroduced in 1986, Turbo-Look sales dropped to

1986 Supersport in Grand Prix White with colour-coded Fuchs alloy wheels.

just 15 in 1986, 30 in 1987, 155 in 1988, and 66 in 1989.

Although the 911 Turbo stayed in production for the European and the RoW markets until 1989, a growing number of discerning European customers, who liked the Turbo for its looks, preferred the more drivable and flexible Carrera engine. This may have been a key factor for Porsche's official recognition of the Turbo-Look as more than just a factory option or marketing tool for America. Hence the official European 'Supersport' designation from 1987 onwards.

Although an ideal option for those who like the look of the 911 Turbo, the Turbo-body Carrera was quite expensive. It cost some DM26,000 more in Germany and $10,000 more in America than the standard Carrera in 1984, rising to DM30,000 and $14,000 more in 1989. When officially named the Supersport in 1987, it was £10,000 more expensive than a Sport Equipment car in the United Kingdom. These prices were, however, considerably less than those of the private coachbuilders attempting to match factory quality, some of whom charged as much as $35,000 for a complete conversion, including the necessary suspension modifications, 917 brakes, callipers, wheels, body and paintwork. Hence, Porsche effectively stole the market back.

The Turbo-Look cars had an additional option to delete the standard aerodynamic front and rear spoilers. These cars were known as 'without spoilers' or 'spoiler delete' under separate option code M470 for 1984, changing to P59 for 1985 to 1987, and P22 for 1988 and 1989. As with the Speedster, revised front quarter panels were incorporated replacing the wraparound chin spoiler. American Turbo-Look Carreras came without the rear engine lid 'Carrera' script logo as standard, whereas the RoW had it fitted as standard, though cars could be ordered without the script as option M498.

The 911 Carrera Supersport was not an independent model, but later Porsche literature has the SSE variant listed under Optional Equipment and says: "For drivers with even more sporting aspirations ..." Being approximately 70kg heavier than the standard Carrera due to wider wheels, tyres and wheelarches, the Turbo-Look aerodynamic drag was also increased due to the larger overall body area. The SSE acceleration figures were slightly lower than a standard Carrera. Test results showed them to be over a second slower to 100mph.

The interior was identical to the standard Carrera, as were key dimensions like wheelbase, length and height. When ordered, the car

American Turbo-Look Carrera with option code M470 – 'without spoilers/spoilers delete'.

The full 911 Turbo aerodynamic front and rear spoilers were fitted to the Turbo-Look and Supersport Carreras.

Left: Two American spec Turbo-Look Coupés. 421MADE is a fitting registration plate as it represents the number of Turbo-Look Coupés imported into the United States during 1984.

had all the standard options available, including the 491 code, and these were listed in the handbook, in the front boot compartment, and, for American cars only, on a window sticker (which also referred to '930 performance body/chassis'). The body, which was 123 millimetres wider than standard, incorporated standard doors, boot lid and bonnet lid, as well as the wider front and rear wings, wider 'shaped' bumpers, a fully wraparound front chin spoiler and the Turbo rear wing.

Technically, the engine (types 930/20, 930/21, 930/25 and 930/26) and transmission (type 915) were the same as the standard Carrera. From 1987 onwards, the Turbo-Look also benefited from the much improved G50 gearbox and hydraulic clutch mechanism.

The suspension design and fitments were uprated to match the 911 Turbo. 18.8mm torsion bars and a 22mm anti-roll bar were fitted at the front, and 26mm torsion bars and a 20mm anti-roll bar were fitted at the rear, although larger 27 millimetre rear torsion bars were introduced with the G50 cars. It also had larger semi-trailing arms at the rear; some 50mm wider than standard.

16 inch Fuchs alloy wheels were standard for the Turbo-Look. The front and rear rim widths being 7, 8 and 9 inches wide respectively. There were no 'Turbo-Look' identifying body markings used other than the standard 'Carrera' or 'Porsche' badges on the nose, rear light cluster and engine cover.

As an option to the standard Carrera, the 491 code was probably the most comprehensive and certainly the most expensive. Porsche was keen to offer the more discerning driver the latest styling, wider and arguably more aggressive looking Turbo aesthetics. Although straight line performance was slightly slower, the brakes were considerably better than those on the standard Carrera.

The Carrera Turbo Look (option M491) replaced the 911 Turbo from 1984 to 1986 in America. This was due to restrictive emission control laws dating from 1980.

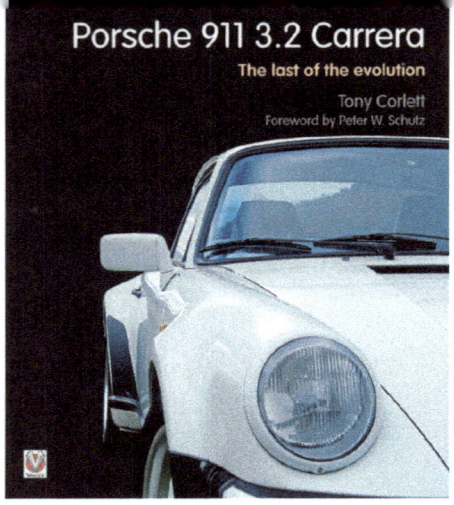

Chapter 6

M637 Club Sport: Blueprinted

India Red Fuchs wheels as standard on a United Kingdom specification Club Sports.

The Club Sport (CS) was a lightened and simplified variant of the 3.2 Carrera Coupé. Porsche took an already established and well engineered package and, in the face of some criticism that the 911s were 'too padded', produced a lighter and more sporting car to suit its more competitive customers. Two areas of the standard Carrera Coupé were targeted in order to create a car that was special enough to have it's own name; weight reduction and engine balance, the latter resulting in a 'blueprinted' version of the standard 3.2 Carrera engine, specially designated with 'SP' on the crankcase. The Club Sport was introduced in 1987 to provide a more sporting road car suitable for regular track use or, with further modifications, to form the basis of a club racer.

The Club Sport was a reminder that the 911 was still a raw sports car that could be used and enjoyed on the road during the week, yet could be raced on a track in club events at the weekend. Whilst the 959 demonstrated Porsche's advanced technical prowess with sophisticated new systems that would be incorporated into the forthcoming new generation cars, the Club Sport, in contrast, was the essence of a purely functional sports Coupé, in keeping with the spirit of the revered 1973 Carrera 2.7RS.

Based on the 1987 Coupé which was already fitted with the improved G50 gearbox and hydraulic clutch, the Club Sport came with none of the luxury items associated with the standard Coupé. The specification put the emphasis on the critical areas of weight reduction and optimising the performance and handling characteristics. It carried the lightened chassis specification 'M637', and the chassis numbers started at 105000 for years 1987 (H) and 1988 (J). However, the 1989 (K) cars were only available by special order, and the chassis numbers ran in sequence with the standard Carrera Coupé.

The exact specification varied slightly for different markets, but the principal modifications to the standard Carrera Coupé included:

M637 chassis specification
• Deletion of electric sunroof
• Deletion of Carrera logo on engine lid
• Deletion of rear and sidewall trim panels
• Deletion of central locking
• Deletion of rear wiper
• Deletion of front fog lights
• Deletion of headlamp washers
• Deletion of PVC underseal
• Deletion of heavy duty sound insulation (except for engine and roof lining)
• Deletion of passenger sun visor
• Deletion of boot/engine courtesy lights
• Deletion of glove box lock (some markets only)
• Deletion of coat hooks
• Deletion of rear speakers
• Deletion of lids for door storage compartments
• Replacement of electric window lifts with mechanical winders
• Replacement of electric front seats with manually adjusted sports seats

Official factory promotional photograph of the 1987 Club Sport.

A typical UK specification Carrera Club Sport in Grand Prix White with India Red trim.

The Carrera Club Sport was almost identical to the standard Sport-equipped Coupé. Visual differences include the lack of front fog lamps and the inclusion of flank or front wing decals.

- Replacement of rear seats and belts with carpeted rear shelf
- Simplified manual heating system
- Simplified radio system
- Simplified, lightweight wiring harness
- Lightened, non-recoil bumper mountings
- Lightened space-saver spare wheel
- Fuel tank without PVC coating
- Modified, sculpted front bumper to admit more air to oil cooler

Engine
- Manufactured to 'blueprint' specification
- Lightened, hollow intake valve stems
- Modified Bosch DME, extending peak revs from 6520rpm to 6840rpm
- Modified engine/gearbox mounts
- Modified air cleaner with carbon canister plug
- Crankcase and cylinder head stamped 'SP' to differentiate the Club Sport engine from the standard Carrera unit

Transmission
- Limited slip differential
- Short throw gear lever
- Revised 4th and 5th gear ratios

Suspension, wheels, tyres
- Bilstein sports dampers
- 6Jx16 front and 7Jx16 rear Fuchs forged alloy wheels
- 205/55 VR front and 225/50 VR rear tyres

Aerodynamics
- Front and rear Sport Equipment spoilers

Although there was no special racing technology used, the engine components were carefully selected and matched from the standard parts so as to provide uniform output and reliability. This, together with the other subtle engine modifications and the lighter chassis, provided a power to weight ratio of over 200bhp/tonne.

Although the standard Sport Equipment Coupé performance figures were officially quoted for the Club Sport, it is widely accepted that these cars, in European specification, produced over 240bhp. A revised version of the standard Bosch Motronic injection and engine management system was used which raised the peak revs from 6520rpm to 6840rpm. It came with a short-shift gear linkage and a limited slip differential as standard. Apart from a slightly modified air intake, Porsche chose not to revise the standard throttle bodies and exhaust system.

The brakes and suspension were identical to the Sport Equipment but the Club Sport ran Bilstein Sport dampers as standard.

Opposite: The Club Sport had a limited production run from 1987 to 1989 of just 340 cars in total. Although Porsche officially produced the Club Sport in 1989, they were not specifically noted, unlike the 1987 and 1988 cars which had chassis numbers starting at 5000. The +5000 designation was reserved for the Speedster in 1989, so the Club Sport was produced within the usual Coupé chassis numbers.

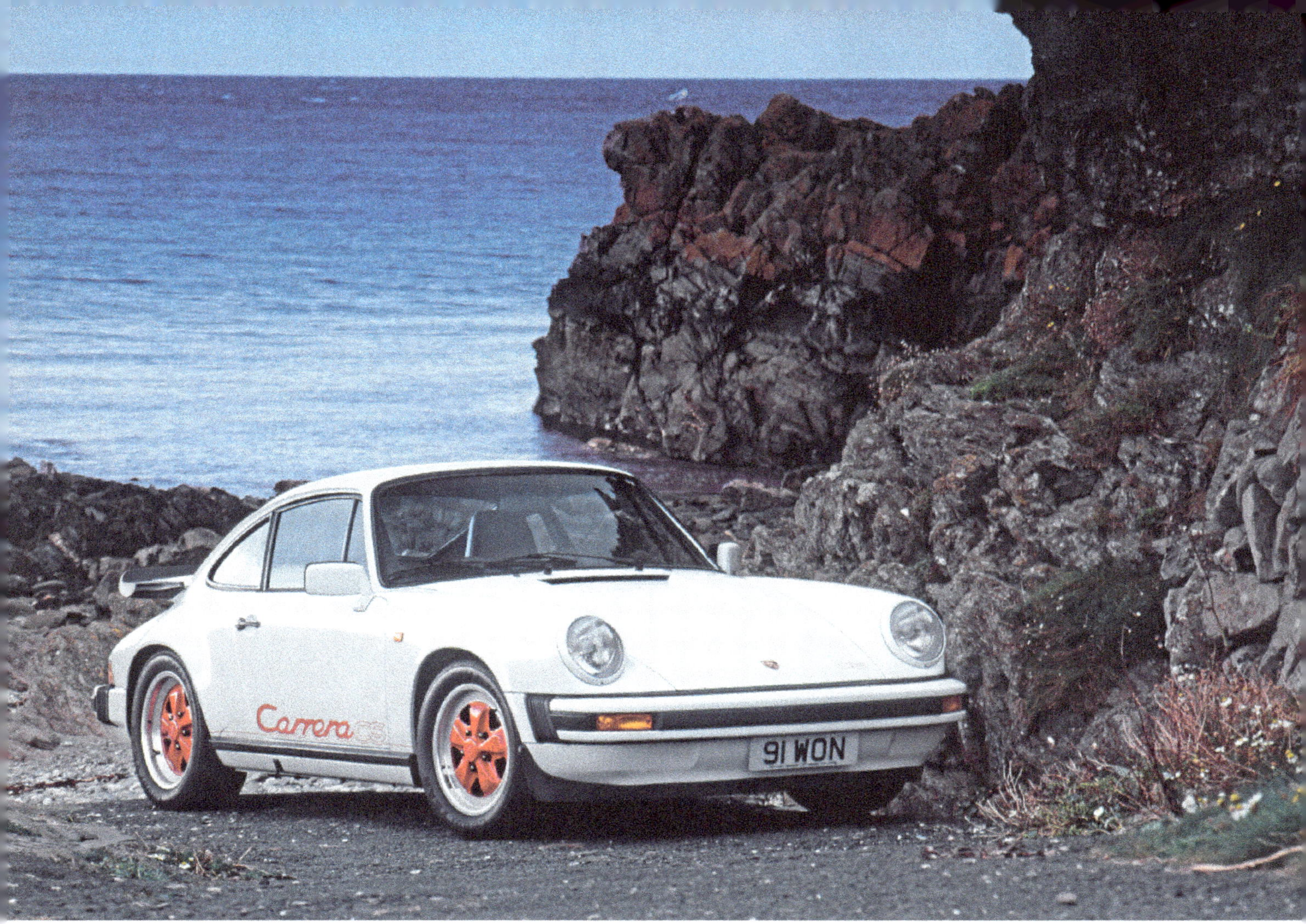
91 WON
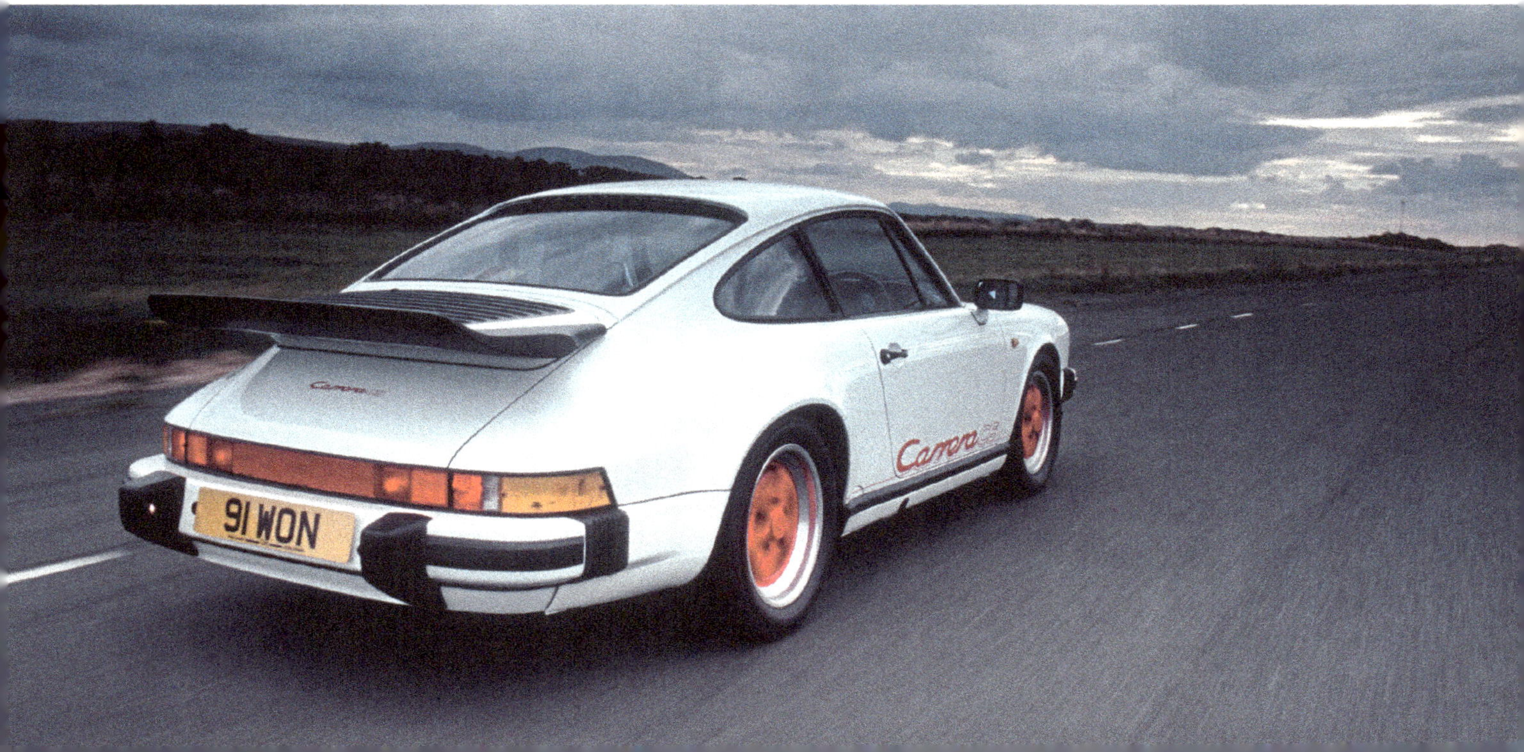
91 WON

Great White meets great white.

Performance figures for the Club Sport were as follows:

0 - 30mph	2.0 seconds
0 - 50mph	4.0 seconds
0 - 60mph	5.1 seconds
0 - 100mph	13.1 seconds
0 - 120mph	19.6 seconds
50 - 70 (5th gear)	7.4 seconds
50 - 70 (4th gear)	5.6 seconds
Maximum speed	152.1mph

The Club Sport's straight line performance was slightly better than the standard Carrera's, and it was quicker than the 2.7RS and the, then new and very quick, 250bhp 944 Turbo SE. In addition, the reduced weight and better chassis specification provided much sharper dynamics, enabling the Club Sport to handle with greater agility. The Club Sport also benefited from improved braking and lower fuel consumption.

The kerb weight of the Club Sport was quoted at 1160kg, a claimed saving of 50kg over a standard Carrera Coupé. However, it is likely that most European Club Sports weighed closer to 1135kg, and were, in fact, around 75kg lighter than a typically-specified Carrera Coupé with Sports Equipment.

The precise specification of the production Club Sports varied slightly for different markets. In the majority of cases, they were offered in a choice of colours, mostly non-metallic, with discreet CS Club Sport graphics on the left-hand front wing. However, all but one of the UK Club Sports were finished in distinctive Grand Prix White, with Indian Red wheel centres and prominent red Carrera CS script along the lower flanks of each door, mimicking the Carrera 2.7RS from 1973. The exception was exactly the opposite, finished in Indian Red with Grand Prix White detailing.

There was a choice of interior trim colours, although most cars had black leatherette with pinstripe cloth front seats.

Despite the sporting designation, it was possible to specify additional equipment from the options list. Most cars remained standard, though, as a higher specification would have contradicted the basic, sporting nature of the car.

A total of only 340 Club Sports were built by the factory, 81 in 1987, 169 in 1988 and 90 in 1989. Just 53 right-hand drive examples were imported into the United Kingdom and only 28 'federalised' examples were imported into America during 1988 and 1989. It is thought that all 81 cars from 1987 remained in Germany.

The Club Sport was a noisier, less comfortable car, with little really to distinguish it from the normal roadgoing, sport-equipped Carrera. Side by side, the Club Sport and the Coupé with Sports Equipment were identical, apart from the additional 'CS' decals and the absence of front fog lights on the former.

When the Club Sport was launched it received mixed reaction. The 1980s had seen a new generation of Porsche customer, with new wealth emerging from a booming economy. Many of these customers wanted to be part of the 911's sporting heritage, but couldn't live without the creature comforts of air-conditioning, electric windows, sunroof, central locking, etc. Purists were disappointed that the Club Sport hadn't gone further, with lightened panels and glass, and an even more basic specification in keeping with the original Carrera 2.7RS 'lightweight'. But this was late in the Carrera 3.2's life cycle, and an 'RS' variant couldn't be justified. Instead, the Club Sport bridged the gap.

A most desirable 911 variant, the Club Sport offered arguably the best marriage of 911 road car to 911 race car, and with it came all the flavour of a raw 911 with just a hint of sophistication. It's a shame that the 911 3.2 Carrera never made it to RS status, but the Club Sport filled the gap admirably and was, perhaps, in many ways, more appropriate for the time.

The Carrera Club Sport was a lightweight version of a Sport-equipped Coupé. Some 50kg lighter, the Club Sport was designed to offer occasional club racing. This is a typical United Kingdom specification RHD car in Grand Prix White with red 'Carrera CS' decals. There are thought to have been only 53 right-hand drive Club Sports imported into the United Kingdom.

This is an American specification LHD Club Sport in black: it's thought to be one of only three.

Distinctive Club Sport graphic on the front left fender of American Club Sports.

Thought to be the only Diamond Blue Club Sport in the world, this is a 1989 American specification Carrera with the later type 930/26 low compression 217bhp engine. There are thought to have been only 28 'federalised' Club Sports imported into America.

A row of American specification Club Sports. Whilst all but one of the United Kingdom specification Club Sports were Grand Prix White with red trim, American specification cars came in a variety of colours. They also did not carry the flank script, but did have a distinctive Club Sport logo on the front left fender.

An American Club Sport in Silver with black headlamp surrounds. Note the side reflectors within the front bumper forming an extension to the indicator lens for US specification Carreras.

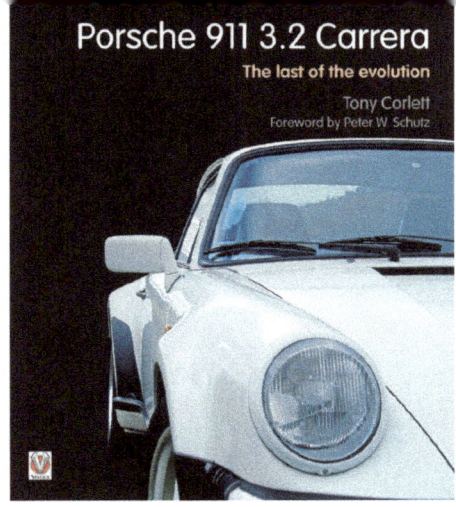

Chapter 7

M503 911 Speedster: Bott's creation

The 911 Speedster was introduced in 1989 as a radically different Carrera, aimed at capturing the spirit of the historic 356 Speedsters. Drawn from the traditional Porsche 'Speedster' design, it came with a lowered windscreen and cabriolet roof. It was also available in both wide body and narrow body versions, the most popular being the wide body or Turbo-Look M491 option.

Soon after the launch of the Cabriolet in 1981, Porsche recognised the (largely American) requirement

Official 1989 Porsche promotional photograph showing a Speedster with a standard body.

Official 1989 Porsche promotional photograph showing the Speedster with a Turbo-Look body.

for a simple, light, and fine weather-use 911. Originally based on an SC chassis, the 911 Speedster made its way into production in 1983 under the direction of Prof. Helmuth Bott. Bott developed the prototype 911 Speedster in a little under six weeks, but it was subsequently shelved and locked away. This car became known as 'Bott's Speedster'.

Officially launched at the 1987 Frankfurt Motor Show, it wasn't until 1989 that Bott's creation was allowed to venture forward. By that stage it was considered unsuitable for production without some modifications, which included a taller windscreen capable of having a windscreen wiper fitted. The 911 Speedster finally went into production in 1988 as a 1989 'K' programme car, within the body of the 3.2 Carrera but without the aerodynamic front and rear spoilers.

Knowing by then that the 911 Carrera production run was due to end in 1989, Porsche still chose to introduce the Speedster as a 3.2 Carrera. Perhaps this was a pre-launch special for the eventual 964 chassis or, more likely, an easier adaptation of Bott's SC based car. Either way, only 2104 3.2 based Speedsters were produced in 1989, of which only 161 were narrow bodied and only 139 were right-hand drive.

The wide body Speedster was effectively a Supersport in non-sport guise. Without an aerodynamic front chin spoiler, two outer valance quarter panels were fitted to the Speedster in order to make up the width in the wider front wings and wheelarches. These quarter panels also incorporated the standard recessed fog lights.

Strictly a two-seater, the Speedster was a great combination of the Club Sport and the Cabriolet. As with the original 356 Speedsters, this 911 aimed to capture the essence of open top

The Speedster was a lowered variant of the Carrera Cabriolet. The brainchild of Helmuth Bott, the Speedster was developed and shelved in 1983, but was later shown at the 1987 Frankfurt Motor Show and went into production in 1989 as a limited run. The Carrera Speedster was the only 911 Speedster made, following in the spirit of the original 356 Speedsters.

The Speedster 'humps'.

motoring and, to some extent, was never designed to have the soft top raised. The Speedster looked best with the roof down, keeping the low windscreen and the 'speedster' humps prominent.

The Speedster was the Club Sport alternative for the Cabriolet lover and, with that, came a spirit of the traditional open top roadster. The windscreen was designed to be unscrewed and replaced by a small aero-screen in front of the driver for track events. However, even though the windscreen could be removed, Porsche never produced the aero-screen. The seats were lowered to offer better headroom with the lowered roof line and, as with the Club Sport, a lot of the unnecessary weighty items were removed.

Porsche designed a radically lower windscreen, and raked it some 5 degrees flatter than the standard screen, which was fitted within a slimline aluminium structure. The quarter-lights were also removed from the standard Cabriolet doors. To capture the original 'Speedster' image, two humps were placed directly behind the front seats, over the area where the rear seats would ordinarily have been, and across the cabriolet roof aperture at the rear of the car. This created a very low sweeping effect. The Speedster

Next two pages: The Speedster was designed for the sunshine. An emergency folding roof was provided, but came with a disclaimer from Porsche that the roof was not entirely weatherproof. The roof was stowed under the 'humps' and was raised manually.

'humps' were moulded in polyurethane and colour matched to the body.

In reality, the Speedster was a lowered Cabriolet, albeit that the unpretentious soft-roof was neither lined nor electrically operated. The Speedster was designed for sunny climates and, although it did have

The Speedster cockpit had lowered windscreen and no side quarter-lights.

a roof, this was neither effective in keeping weather out, nor easy to raise and collapse. The roof nestled below the Speedster humps when stowed. In raising the roof, the hump panel hinged backward and the roof then hinged forward, from where the bottom of the 'B' post would normally be located, allowing the hump panel to be lowered again. The roof was then pulled backward over the hump panel and forward to the top of the windscreen and clipped into place, forming a taut cover. Although the Speedster looked tidy with its roof up, the roof wasn't completely weatherproof, nor did very little in reducing wind noise and, with very low sides, it obstructed the driver's lateral vision. It's clear that this car was never intended to be used with its roof up. In fact, Porsche made prospective owners sign a weather damage waiver prior to purchase.

This 911 variant was never designed to be practical, nor to sell in its thousands. Instead, it represented a pure fashion statement that only Porsche could capture. It was a great example of eccentric motoring for those who wanted to stand out in a crowd, and captured the essence of the much loved 356 predecessors.

The Speedster was probably *the* jewel in the Carrera crown and fitting that it should see out the final days of the last factory-designated 911. It was a wonderful variant and we should be very thankful that it was manufactured at all, let alone as part of the 3.2 Carrera production run.

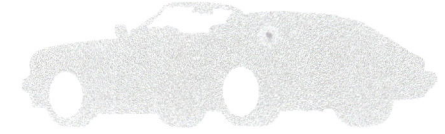

The Speedster was available with a standard or Turbo-Look body and without the aerodynamic front and rear spoilers. The Turbo-Look option incorporated an infill lower front quarter panel up to the front wheelarches.

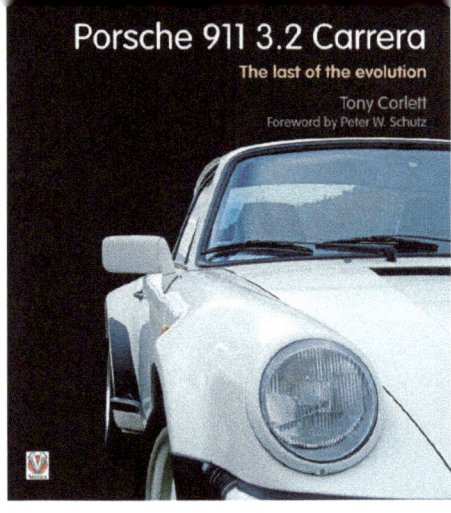

Chapter 8

The engine - type 930

The Carrera engine was available in two basic guises, the type 930/20 and 930/26 with a compression ratio of 10.3:1, and type 930/21 and 930/25, with a compression ratio of 9.5:1.

Derived from the RS 3.0, the 930 had a die-cast aluminium crankcase, 95mm diameter Nikasil cylinders, an aluminium camshaft box (the camshafts running on four bearings), forged pistons cooled directly by oil squirted from crankcase jets, forged connecting rods, and a forged steel crankshaft. The crankshaft ran on eight main bearings, increased from seven with the revised 3.3-litre Turbo type 930/60.

The improved type 930/60 3.3-litre Turbo engine (type 930/66 from 1983) formed the basis of the SC type 930/03 and, subsequently, the 3.2 type 930/20.

The use of Nikasil is an important factor in the Carrera engine as it provided a substantial level of protection to the cylinder bores. Nikasil is an exceptionally hard surface nickel and silicone carbide coating, normally less than 0.1 millimetre thick, which is applied directly to the aluminium bore. Within the nickel coating are particles of silicon carbide, less than 4 microns in size, making up something like 4 per cent of the Nikasil coating and forming adhesion points for oil collection. An extremely tough surface with low friction was achieved, ensuring excellent cylinder lubrication and longevity.

Developed in the early nineteen-eighties, the original 3164cc flat-six engines were twin turbo-charged, developing some 700bhp, and were used in limited numbers in race cars only. These original development engines used the crankshaft from the 930 Turbo and the cylinder bores of the SC, offering a 74.4mm stroke and a 95mm bore. Porsche actually went even further, using 100mm bores with a capacity of 3.5 litres and, although tried and tested, these never made it into production.

The 3.2-litre naturally-aspirated Carrera engine was, therefore, a natural development of the 911 power plant. However, without the advanced development of the Bosch Motronic engine management system, it may have been compromised in terms of the power boost falling foul of increased fuel consumption. The two main elements worked well together and Porsche engineers produced a mighty package with little or no compromise.

Together with the capacity increase over the predecessor's 3.0-litre engine, the 3.2 engine had one other major improvement. The timing chain tensioner cylinders were permanently fed with oil from the engine, thus preventing failure (a regular and expensive problem with earlier 911 engines). This was seen as a major step forward and, in many ways, made the 3.2 Carrera engine almost totally reliable. Another major change was the size increase for the inlet and exhaust ports, although the same size valves were used. That increase, together with the use of a larger diameter exhaust system, meant that the engine breathed more efficiently, producing 73bhp per litre, compared to the 68bhp per litre of the earlier 3.0-litre engine.

The Carrera was produced with four different 930 flat-six air-cooled engine units. With a capacity of 3164cc, the power output was a strong 231bhp, reduced to 207 or 217 for the American market in lower compression format. This is a Porsche 1986 promotional photograph of a type 930/20 with optional air-conditioner pump.

The modifications over the 3.0-litre engine brought the 3.2 dry engine weight up to 219kg, compared to the 190kg of the 3.0 litre. Although the 3.2 engine weighed over 35kg heavier than the original 901 engine, it could still be housed in an original 901 engine bay without modification to either.

With its new engine and revised ratios in the 915 gearbox, the 1984 930/20 European Carrera hit the road running. Porsche claimed a top speed of 152mph and a staggering fuel consumption figure of 41.6mpg at a steady 55mph. At a steady 75mph, the Carrera's efficiency really showed, with Porsche claiming 31.4mpg, a truly remarkable return for a car with such performance reserves.

For the American, Canadian and Japanese markets, all running on lead-free fuel, the 930/20 engine was fitted with flatter pistons and re-named 930/21. It had a lower compression ratio (9.5:1) and was tuned to run on 91 octane fuel. This engine, which had a three-way catalytic converter and lambda sensor but maintained the same type of engine management system and valve timing, produced only 207bhp at 5900rpm. The type 930/21 was replaced by the type 930/25 in 1987, to coincide with the new G50 gearbox. The new type 930/25 used a different Motronic engine management system and ran on 95 octane fuel, and power output increased to 217bhp.

Engine type 930/26 was specifically introduced in 1985 for the Swiss market only. Although exactly the same as the 930/20 except for the inclusion of an air pump blowing into the exhaust ports, the power and torque were identical to that of the 930/20.

The type 930/20 engine ran for the entire life of the Carrera and was sold throughout the world except for America, Canada, Japan and Switzerland. Type 930/26 ran from 1985 to 1989 for the Swiss market only. The low compression type 930/21 ran from 1984 to 1986, and the type 930/25 ran from 1987 to 1989 for America, Canada and Japan. Later 930/20 engines were also fitted with three-way catalytic converters and Lambda sensors, for markets such as Germany, where government tax incentives were offered for cleaner emissions.

Apart from the inclusion of chrome-plated valve stems (from 1986) and the Club Sport 'blueprinted' engine specification, the type 930/20 engine didn't change.

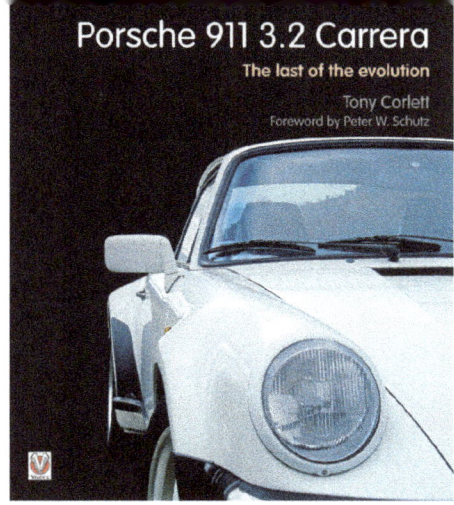

Chapter 9

Ignition and fuel injection

Bosch Motronic ML 3.1

Porsche maximised the performance of the Carrera engine by way of an effective ignition system, providing smooth delivery of power, optimum fuel efficiency, and minimum exhaust emissions. Very much a complete solution, the fuel injection and flat-six engine worked in total harmony, having undergone exhaustive testing with the aim of achieving a power plant of almost perfect proportions.

Porsche retained the tried and tested Bosch petrol injection system, but upgraded to the Motronic system (Bosch L-Jetronic with Digital Motor Electronics - DME) on the Carrera, a type of fuel injection commonly referred to as a pulsed injection system.

This fuel injection system sprayed fuel into the intake manifold when required in the combustion cycle. This way, the fuel delivery was accurately controlled to achieve the most efficient stoichiometric air/fuel ratio of 14/7 (mass of air/mass of fuel). The stoichiometric or 'theoretical combustion' is the ideal combustion process during which the fuel is burned completely. A complete combustion is a process which burns all the carbon (C) to (CO_2), all hydrogen (H) to (H_2O), and all sulphur (S) to (SO_2). If there are any unburned components in the exhaust gas the combustion process is incomplete.

The Motronic setup incorporated an engine management system that controlled the ignition and fuel injection, enabling the Carrera engine to function at its optimum level. The Motronic system timed and metered the fuel and dictated when to fire the spark to create combustion at exactly the correct time. The DME computed input from various sensors in the engine (engine speed was measured from the rpm sensor, the amount of air being induced into the engine was measured from the airflow sensor, the exhaust gasses were measured by an oxygen sensor and additional information was gained from the timing and cylinder head sensors). The DME then calculated the optimum ignition timing and fuel delivery to produce the most horsepower with the least amount of emissions.

Constant monitoring and instantaneous adjustment to the fuel/air mixture and ignition timing to over four thousand possible combinations produced durability, reliability and performance without compromise. The DME computer's chip contained a data map based upon dynometer and emissions tests carried out by Porsche. At any split second, the DME could read all of the data input from the engine sensors, compare it to the original data map, and dictate how much fuel to deliver and when to fire the ignition.

The Motronic system also controlled the maximum engine revolutions, cutting off the fuel supply at 6520rpm, and an idling speed stabilization function ensured an even-running engine.

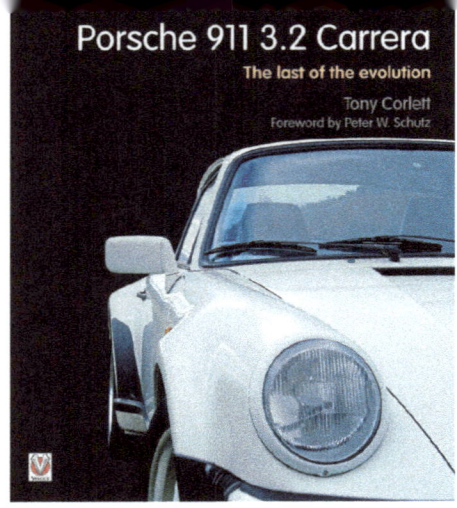

Chapter 10

Transmission - 915 to G50

Derived from the Porsche type 916 racing gearbox, the type 915 unit was first introduced in 1971 as a four-speed unit, before being uprated to a five-speed. Originally cast in magnesium alloy for a lighter casing, from 1978 onwards the type 915 was cast in aluminium for greater strength. This laid a good foundation for the powerful 3.2 output in 1984, though the type 915 was stretched to its limits.

For the 3.2 engine, the type 915 gearbox was fitted with an oil cooler, and the fourth and fifth gear pinions were modified. This was to keep the gearbox oil cooler under the higher power and torque load of the type 930/20 engine. The oil cooler was mounted on the left side of the gearbox housing just ahead of the driveshafts.

Ironically, the problems associated with cooling the oil in the type 915 gearbox effectively caused its demise in 1986. As well as being an expensive solution, Porsche realized that its own synchronizers, durable and reliable as they were, were not going to cope with the increasing gear shifting forces, so it chose the tried and tested 924/944 Audi-based Borg-Warner synchronisers for an all new gearbox for 1987.

The new G50 gearbox, with the Borg-Warner synchronisers and without the need for an oil cooler, was produced by Getrag, an independent manufacturer, in 1987. The new gearbox was a completely new design and had great potential in terms of torque loading, so much so, in fact, that Porsche used the new G50 gearbox in its 911 Turbo in 1989, the very first five-speed gearbox to be used in a 911 Turbo. A further development ensured that, if required, Porsche could save weight with the G50 by going back to a magnesium housing, though an aluminium housing went into production.

The switch from type 915 to type G50 was an important step, and one which carried with it a whole new approach to gear change. The G50 unit was a far more efficiently-designed unit, and substantially improved ease of operation and gear shift throw.

Several gearbox combinations were offered throughout the life of the Carrera. From 1984 to 1986, types 915-67, 915-68, 915-69, 915-70, 915-72 and 915-73 were used and, from 1987 to 1989 with the G50 gearbox, types G50-00, G50-01 and G50-02 were used.

From 1984 to 1986 with the type 915 gearbox, Porsche used a cable-operated clutch and plate diameter of 225mm. For the type G50 gearbox from 1987 to 1989, the clutch was uprated to hydraulic operation and the plate diameter was increased to 240mm, the same size as that used in the 911 Turbo.

Gearbox type: 915-72/915-67/915-69		
Final drive	8:31	3.875:1
1st gear	11:35	3.182:1
2nd gear	18:33	1.833:1
3rd gear	23:29	1.261:1
4th gear	29:28	0.966:1
5th gear	38:29	0.763:1
Maximum rpm in 5th gear	6520	

Gearbox type: 915-73/915-68/915-70		
Final drive	8:31	3.875:1
1st gear	11:35	3.182:1
2nd gear	18:32	1.778:1
3rd gear	23:29	1.261:1
4th gear	26:26	1.000:1
5th gear	38:30	0.789:1
Maximum rpm in 5th gear	6520	

Gearbox type: G50-00: Europe and rest of world (inc. Club Sport)		
Final drive	9:31	3.444:1
1st gear	12:42	3.500:1
2nd gear	17:35	2.059:1
3rd gear	22:31	1.409:1
4th gear	27:29	1.074:1
5th gear	36:31	0.861:1
Maximum rpm in 5th gear	6520	

Gearbox type: G50-01: USA, Canada and Japan (inc. Club Sport)		
Final drive	9:31	3.444:1
1st gear	12:42	3.500:1
2nd gear	17:35	2.059:1
3rd gear	22:31	1.409:1
4th gear (Lower)	32:36	1.125:1
5th gear (Lower)	36:32	0.889:1
Maximum rpm in 5th gear	6520	

Gearbox type: G50-02: Switzerland		
Final drive	9:31	3.444:1
1st gear (Higher)	13:41	3.154:1
2nd gear (Higher)	19:36	1.895:1
3rd gear (Higher)	24:32	1.333:1
4th gear (Higher)	28:29	1.036:1
5th gear	36:31	0.861:1
Maximum rpm in 5th gear	6520	

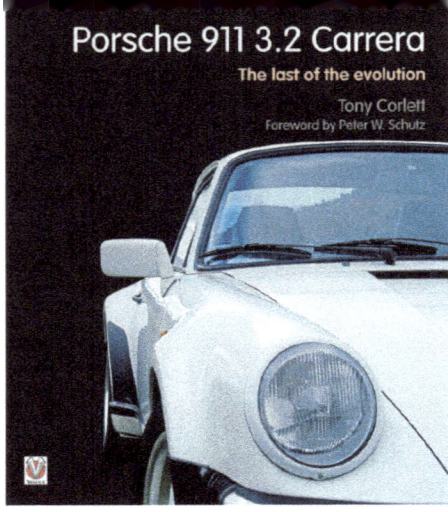

Chapter 11

Suspension

Fully independent to all corners, the 911 Carrera was weighted on torsion bars all round, positioned longitudinally at the front and laterally at the rear. This basic torsion bar design remained unchanged from 1963 to 1989.

The 911 torsion bars were engineered to operate with resistance to a turning moment. That turning moment was applied to the torsion bars via leverage from lower wishbones at the front, and the trailing or radius arms at the rear. Whereas the front wishbones operated sideways, the rear trailing arms operated backwards. An axle control arm was fitted at the rear which picked up the trailing arm and lower damper mounting and ran back towards the middle of the car, pivoting off the floorpan. For 1984 and 1985, the factory standard torsion bar diameter at the front was 18.8mm and the rear was 24mm. From 1986 to 1989, the factory standard torsion bar diameter at the front was 18.8mm and the rear was 25mm.

The entire weight of the car was taken through the turning moment on the torsion bars, and the ride heights were dependent upon the splines within the rigid housings of the torsion bar. Secondary to the torsion bars and wishbones/trailing arms were the dampers, otherwise described as self-levelling, hydro-pneumatic suspension struts. These provided the damped stiffness between the lower mounting point of the control arm at the rear, or wishbones at the front, and the rigid top fixing point of the body. The damper or strut provided the level of stiffness required for varying types of driving styles or comfort. Between the torsion bars and the dampers, the 911 Carrera suspension set up was quite simple. From 1984 to 1989, the factory standard damper was either Boge for the comfort setting or Bilstein for the sport setting.

At the front of the car, the torsion bars were housed within the wishbone or transverse control arm, fixed at the very front to a light alloy crossmember which tied both left and right wishbones together. At the rear of the car, the torsion bars were housed within the floorpan, and ran out towards the side of the car where they connected to the trailing arm. A distinctive body feature of the 911 was the two circular rear torsion bar removal plugs which were positioned in the lower skirt line in front of the rear wheelarches. Removing these allowed access for removal and replacement of the rear torsion bars.

There were only eight main suspension bushes in the entire suspension. Two on each corner, one at either end of the wishbones at the front, and two at the pivot point of the control arms to the floorpan at the rear.

Anti-roll bars were fitted to the front and the rear of the car. These were each fixed through four rubber bushes which were the only ancillary suspension bushes on the car. For 1984 and 1985, the factory standard anti-roll bar diameter was 20mm at the front and 18mm at the rear. From 1986 to 1989, the factory standard anti-roll bar diameter was 22mm at the front and 21mm at the rear.

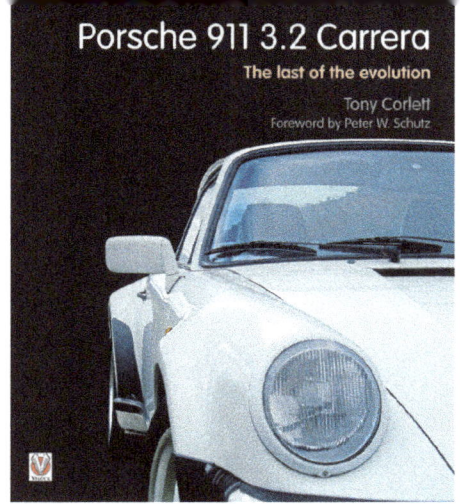

Chapter 12

Fuchs Felge

In the nineteen-sixties, German industrialist Otto Fuchs produced the earliest forged aluminium wheels. These, officially known as '*Fuchs Felge*' in German and 'Fuchs Alloy' in English, went on to become one of the distinctive 'trademarks' of the 911. More recently referred to as the '*Flügel-Rad*' or 'Vane-Type', the word 'Fuchs' is used to describe the wheel synonymous with Porsche 911s. Otto Fuchs KG went on to produce forged wheels for many other manufacturers, but the name 'Fuchs' remains as sole description for the most famous and distinctive Porsche wheel of all.

The forging process is basically a method of shaping heated metal by compression. The Fuchs process for the 911 *Fuchs Felge* starts with a single aluminium alloy billet (aluminium, silicon, magnesium and manganese) before being pressured into the wheel shape with a massive press. This single-billet-forged process provided a very strong wheel which performed with little or no distortion about the hub.

The Fuchs alloy was phased out at the end of Carrera production in 1989, never again to be used by Porsche. It was replaced by the light alloy pressure cast Design 90 and Cup alternatives on the 964. There were good engineering reasons why Porsche dropped the people's favourite wheel, and in some ways the more modern approach to alloys suited the new era of 964 design.

Fuchs offsets:
  6J x 15 H2 36.0mm
  7J x 15 H2 23.3mm
  8J x 15 H2 10.6mm
  9J x 15 H2 3mm

  6J x 16 H2 36.0mm
  7J x 16 H2 23.3mm
  8J x 16 H2 10.6mm
  9J x 16 H2 15mm

The Fuchs forging process shaped the wheel from one single aluminium alloy billet, to the final shape, under compression. This official Fuchs image shows five random stages during compression from the billet on the left to the final wheel on the right.

A typical forged Fuchs alloy wheel. The name Fuchs has become synonymous with the Porsche 911.

FUCHS

Chapter 13

Chassis numbers

WPO ZZZ 91 Z X S 1 Y NNNN

WPO	World manufacturer's code: 'Porsche'	
ZZZ	Replaced with ABO or EBO codes for USA models only, body, engine and restraints as follows:	
ABO	A:	Body code USA/CDN: Carrera Coupé
EBO	E:	Body code USA/CDN: Carrera Targa and Cabriolet
	B:	Code for USA engine variants
	O:	Restraint system: O: Belts
91	First two digits of vehicle type (i.e. 91 for all 911s)	
Z	Check character	
X	Model year:	
	E:	1984
	F:	1985
	G:	1986
	H:	1987
	J:	1988
	K:	1989
S	Plant of origin (S = Stuttgart for all 911s)	
1	Last digit of vehicle type (i.e. 1 for all 911 models)	
Y	Code for body:	
	0:	911 Coupé
	2:	911 Coupé USA and Canada
	4:	911 Targa
	5:	911 Cabriolet and Speedster
	6:	911 Targa USA and Canada
	7:	911 Cabriolet and Speedster USA and Canada
NNNN	Sequential chassis number	

Official 1984 Porsche promotional photograph showing from left to right, Targa, Coupé and Cabriolet for the American market.

911 Carrera

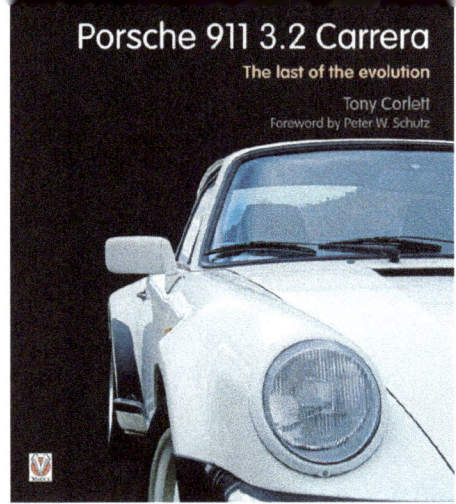

Chapter 14

Factory prices

Prices as quoted from official Porsche price lists (all prices in *deutschmarks*)					
	Coupé*	Targa*	Cabriolet*	Club Sport	Speedster**
1984	68,560	71,660	75,980		
1985	72,000	76,000	82,000		
1986	72,250	79,250	85,250		
1987	80,500	84,600	90,800	80,500	
Cat	82,075	86,175	92,375	82,075	
1988	83,700	88,000	94,200	83,700	110,000
Cat	85,275	89,575	95,775	85,275	111,575
1989	86,000	90,500	96,800		110,000
Cat	87,575	92,075	98,375		111,575

* Standard body without spoilers
* Teledial wheels up to 1988
** Turbo-Look

Sport Equipment options (in *deutschmarks*)				
	F/R Aero Spoilers M473	6x16/7x16 Fuchs M395	7x15/8x15 Fuchs M401	Turbo-Look M491
1984	+2730	+3085	+1850	+25,950
1985	+2850	+3195	+1915	+27,950
1986	+2990	+3355	+2100	+29,350
1987	+2995	+1370	N/A	+29,350
1988	+2995	standard	N/A	+29,750
1989	+2995	standard	N/A	+29,790

Interior equipment options				
	Leather seats M562	Full leather	Customer leather	Air conditioning M559
1984	+1850	+3950	+4350	+3290
1985	+1990	+4090	+5070	+3450
1986	+2130	+4380	+6950	+3620
1987	+2205	+4535	+6990	+3750
1988	+2300	+4715	+7250	+3900
1989	+2300	+4715	+7250	+3900

Exterior paint options		
	Metallic paint	Customer paint
1984	+1380	+2510
1985	+1380	+2650
1986	+1435	+2760
1987	+1485	+2855
1988	+1545	+2965
1989	+1545	+2965

By comparison, in 1984 a Turbo-Look Carrera Coupé would have cost DM94,510 compared to a 911 Turbo Coupé at DM114,000, correspondingly rising to DM115,790 compared to DM138,800 for similar cars in 1989.

Late in 1988, the newly introduced 964 Carrera 4 Coupé could be ordered. It was priced at DM114,500 for availability later in 1989.

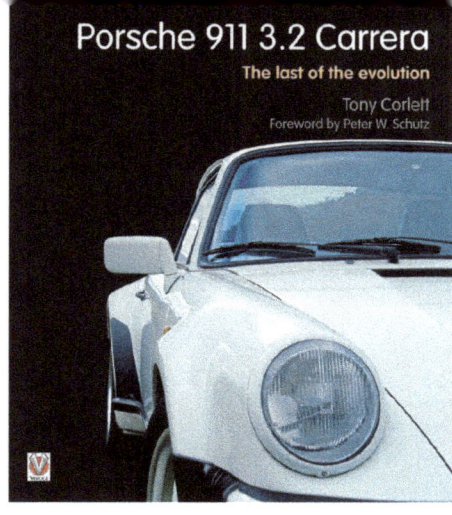

Chapter 15

Manufacture codes

The first code on the identification label is a 'C' code which identifies the market for which the car was produced. This appears not always to have been used on the earlier European cars.

International 'C' codes	
C00	Germany
C02	Equipped with catalytic converter
C03	California type car
C05	France
C07	Italy
C09	Sweden
C10	Swiss version - post 1986 with cat
C11	Austria
C15	Hong Kong
C16	United Kingdom
C20	Holland
C22	Belgium
C23	Australia
C24	Greece
C26	Singapore/South Africa
C32	Saudi Arabia
C36	Canada

Below are examples of standard equipment for UK and USA markets in 1987:

Standard UK Specification for 1987 (C16)*
5-speed manual transmission
Forged alloy road wheels, black with anti-theft device
Sport shock absorbers
Front and rear anti-roll bars
Front and rear aerodynamic spoilers
Integral front and high intensity rear fog lamps
Brake pad wear indicator
2-stage heated rear window (Coupé and Targa only)
3-speed windscreen wipers, variable intermittent wipe settings with heated,

electrically operated windscreen washers and additional heavy duty windscreen wash system
Internally adjustable headlamps
Headlamp washers
Rear window wiper (Coupé and Targa only)
Impact absorbing bumpers
Electrically operated windows
Central door locking
Tinted, heat insulating glass
Electrically operated sunroof (Coupé only)
Electrically operated roof (Cabriolet only)
Heated, electrically adjustable mirrors for driver and passenger doors
Thermostatic heating control
Electrically adjustable front seats (partial leather)
Leather covered steering wheel (380mm diameter)
Blaupunkt Toronto digital self-seek stereo radio with combined auto-reverse cassette player with Dolby and metal tape facilities, cassette programme search, anti-theft code protection, 4x20 watt output. 8 speaker system (6 on Cabriolet) and integral windscreen aerial

Standard USA Specification for 1987*

Oil cooler, front
Four-wheel independent torsion bar suspension with stabilizer bars, front and rear
Welded, unitary construction; double sided zinc-galvanised body
Dual circuit four-wheel vented disc brakes, power assisted
Forged alloy wheels
Aluminium spare tire rim with space saving tire
Electrically adjustable and heated outside rear-view mirrors
Brake pad wear indicator light
Upshift indicator light
Integrated fog lights
Anti-theft device on wheels
Windshield with graduated tint
Halogen headlights
Heatable windshield washer nozzles
Steel belted radials
Rack and pinion steering
Inertia reel 3-point seat belts, front and lap belts, rear
Driver seat with electric height and backrest adjustment
Reclining bucket seats
Choice of partial leather seats

Leather covered steering wheel
Transistorized tachometer
Trip odometer
Sun visors with covered vanity mirrors
Quartz analog clock
Electric rear window defroster, two stage (Coupé and Targa)
Power windows
Tinted glass all round
Deep cut carpeting
Carpeted luggage compartment
Electric windshield wiper with intermittent wiper cycle
Air conditioning
Blaupunkt Portland digital FM/AM cassette radio
Windshield antenna, 4 loudspeakers, suppression kit

* As listed in official Porsche literature for UK and USA - 1987

It is not unusual on the earlier cars to find only the 'C' code listed in the handbook. Later cars also had further 'M' Option Codes listed as well as the 'C' code.

Option 'M' Codes (Mehrausstattungs Nummer)

Official Porsche 911 Carrera Option List : 1984 to 1989		
M Code	Description	Associated M Code
018	Sport steering wheel with elevated hub	
058	Bumpers with impact absorbers	
070	Tonneau cover - Cabriolet	
139	Seat heating - left	
197	88Ah battery	
220	Locking differential (40%)	
243	Shorter gear shift lever	
261	Passenger side mirror electric plain	528
286	High intensity windscreen washer	
288	Headlight washer	
298	Prepared for unleaded fuel, manual transmission	
326	Radio Blaupunkt Berlin IQR 86/IQR 88	328, 330, 686, 688, 494, 690

Official Porsche 911 Carrera Option List : 1984 to 1989		
M Code	Description	Associated M Code
327	Radio Blaupunkt Köln SQR 23	330, 686, 688
328	Radio Blaupunkt Bremen SQR 45/SQR 46	330, 686, 688, 326, 690
330	Radio Blaupunkt Atlanta SQR 23/Toronto SQR 24/SQR 46	327, 686, 688, 328, 326, 690
340	Seat heating - right	
341	Central locking system	
348	Forged wheels in Grand Prix White	485
379	Series seat, left electrical vertical adjustment	383, 437, 586
380	Series seat, right electrical vertical adjustment	387, 438, 513
383	Sport seat - left	437, 586, 980, 379
387	Sport seat - right	438, 513, 980, 380
395	Light metal wheels forged	401, 455, 491, P59
401	Light metal wheels	395, 455, 491, P59
419	Rear luggage compartment instead of rear seats	
425	Rear wiper	559
430	Rectangular fog light yellow lens	
437	Full power seat - left	383, 379
438	Comfort seat - right	387, 380
439	Electric Cabriolet roof	
451	2 speakers on back shelf	
454	Cruise control	
455	Wheel locks	395, 401, 491
462	Sekuriflex windshield	
463	Clear windshield	567
470	Without spoilers, in conjunction with Turbo-Look	
473	With spoilers	491, P59, P22
474	Sport shock absorbers - Bilstein	491, P59, P22
485	Forged wheels in gold metallic	348
490	Hi-Fi sound system	
491	Turbo-Look	P59, 395, 401, 455, 473, 474, 49
494	Amplifier system	326, 686
496	Prepared for cellular telephone	
498	Without rear model designation	491, P59
513	Lumbar support - right seat	387, 380
526	Cloth door panels	980
528	Passenger side mirror convex	261
533	Alarm system	

Official Porsche 911 Carrera Option List : 1984 to 1989		
M Code	Description	Associated M Code
559	Air conditioner	425
567	Windshield green graduated tint	463
586	Lumbar support - left seat	383, 379
605	Vertical headlight adjustment	
650	Sunroof	
686	Radio Blaupunkt Hamburg SQM 24/ Ludwigsburg SQM 26	327, 330, 688, 328, 326, 494, 690
688	Radio Blaupunkt Boston SQM 23	327, 330, 686, 328, 326, 494
690	Porsche CD-10 with radio	326, 328, 330, 686
975	Velour carpet in luggage compartment	
980	Seat cover ruffled leather	383, 387
P22	Turbo-Look without spoilers	473, 474
P40	Forged wheels	
P59	Without spoilers	491, 395, 401, 473, 474, 498

There were many more Porsche 'M' option codes available but not officially denoted within Porsche literature, option lists and price lists for 1984 to 1989.

Official 1985 Porsche promotional photograph showing a Turbo-Look Cabriolet without front and rear aerodynamic spoilers. Note how the modified front lower quarter panels differ from production models.

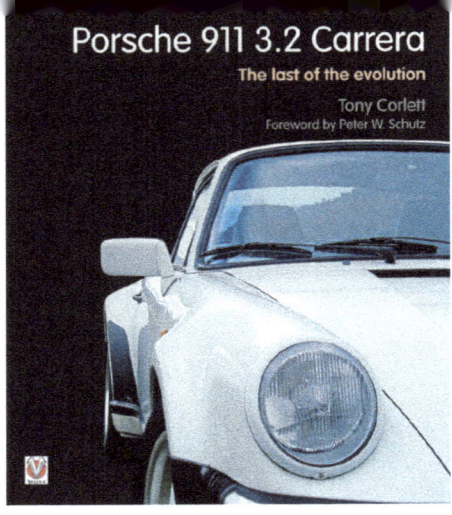

Chapter 16

Colours

Please note that colour reproduction may not be completely accurate.

1983/1984				
Colour	Metallic	Codes		
Grand Prix White		908		P5
India Red		027	L M3A	G8
Black		700	L 041	A1
Alpine White			L 90E	
Pasadena Yellow			L Y1L	
Glacier Blue		32Z		K4
Chiffon White		182		
Pewter	Metallic	956		U3
Platinum	Metallic	655	L M8U	U1
Moss Green	Metallic	20C		Y8
Slate Blue	Metallic	661		X6
Quartz Grey	Metallic	662		X5
Kiln Red	Metallic	811		X3
Ruby Red	Metallic	810	L M3V	X7
Light Bronze	Metallic	966	L M1V	R6
Sapphire	Metallic		L Y5V	
Montego Black	Metallic		L Y9V	
Gemini Grey	Metallic		L Z7Z	
Zermatt Silver	Metallic		L Y7Y	

1985/1986				
Colour	Metallic	Codes		
Grand Prix White		908		P5
India Red		027	L M3A	G1
Black		700	L 041	A1
Alpine White			L 90E	
Marble Grey		673		A8
Pastel Beige		536	LM1N	D4

1985/1986				
Colour	Metallic	Codes		
Dark Blue		347		K5
Nutmeg Brown	Metallic	492		S1
Garnet Red	Metallic	822	L M3Y	S2
Iris Blue	Metallic	33P		S3
Prussian Blue	Metallic	33X		S4
Crystal Green	Metallic	33N	L M6Y	S5
White Gold	Metallic	539		S6
Silver	Metallic	936		S7
Moss Green	Metallic	20C		Y8
Meteor Grey	Metallic	961		Y5
Sapphire	Metallic		L Y5V	
Zermatt Silver	Metallic		L Y7Y	
Mahogany Brown	Metallic		L B8Z	
Kalahari Beige	Metallic		L A1Y	
Slate Grey	Metallic		L Y7U	
Pearl White	Metallic		L OA9	

1987/1988				
Colour	Metallic	Codes		
Grand Prix White		908		P5
Black		700	L 041	A1
Dark Blue		347		K5
Cherry/Carmine Red		80F		
Citrus Yellow		10W		
Ceramic/Caramel Beige		499		
Turquoise		21M		M7
Indian Red		80K	LM3A	G1
Alpine White			L 90E	
Summer Yellow			LM1A	B1
Silver	Metallic	980		S7
Laguna Green	Metallic	35Y		F2
Granite Green	Metallic	699		F3
Nougat Brown	Metallic	40B	L M8V	F4
Diamond Blue	Metallic	697	LM5U	F6
Espresso Brown	Metallic	40D		F5
Navy Blue	Metallic	35V		
Venetian Blue	Metallic	35U		F8
Cassis Red	Metallic	80D		F9
Zermatt Silver	Metallic		L Y7Y	
Slate Grey	Metallic		L Y7U	

1987/1988			
Colour	Metallic	Codes	
Nautit/Ocean Blue	Metallic		L Y5Z
Flamingo	Metallic		L Y4Z
Maraschino Red	Metallic		L Y3V
Almond Beige	Metallic		L Y1Y

1989				
Colour	Metallic	Codes		
Grand Prix White		908		P5
Black		700	L 041	A1
Dark Blue		347		K5
Indian Red		80K		G1
Linen		60M	L MIU	E2
Apricot Beige		548		E4
Murano Green		22C		N6
Alpine White			L 90E	
Silver	Metallic	980		S7
Diamond Blue	Metallic	697		F5
Dove Blue	Metallic	37B	C7	
Stone Grey	Metallic	693		U8
Slate	Metallic	22D		
Velvet Red	Metallic	81L		U6
Linen Grey	Metallic	550		W5
Pine Green	Metallic	22E		W7
Cognac Brown	Metallic	40L		Z7
Salmon/Coral	Metallic	81K		Z9
Zermatt Silver	Metallic		L Y7Y	
Slate Grey	Metallic		L Y7U	
Glacier Blue	Metallic		L Y5U	
Bamboo	Metallic		L Y1Z	
Baltic Blue	Metallic	37B		C7
Forest Green	Metallic	22E		W7

Targa Roof and Cabriolet Hood Colour Codes		
Colour	Code	Model
Dark Brown	V4	Cabriolet
Burgundy	V5	Cabriolet
Mahogany	V6	Cabriolet
Grey Green	V7	Cabriolet
Dark Blue	V8	Cabriolet
Black	V9	Targa & Cabriolet

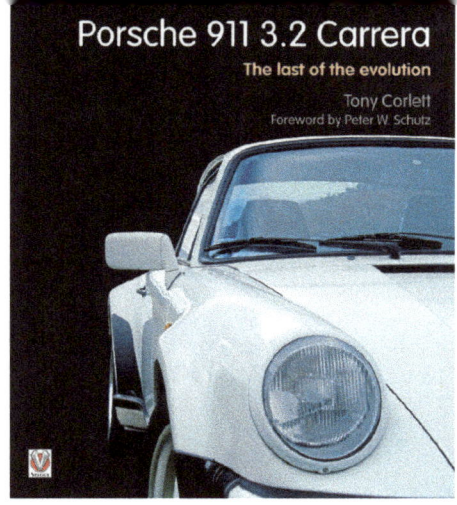

Chapter 17

Official factory production numbers

Model year 1984 (E-Program)		
911 Model	Chassis number range	Production
Carrera Coupé	91 ES 10 0001 - 91 ES 10 4033	3973
Carrera Coupé Japan	91 ES 10 9501 - 91 ES 10 9717	157
Carrera Coupé US and CDN	91 ES 12 0001 - 91 ES 12 2282	2222
Carrera Targa	91 ES 14 0001 - 91 ES 14 1469	1409
Carrera Targa Japan	91 ES 14 9501 - 91 ES 14 9564	4
Carrera Cabriolet	91 ES 15 0001 - 91 ES 15 1835	1775
Carrera Cabriolet Japan	91 ES 15 9501 - 91 ES 15 9577	17
Carrera Targa US and CDN	91 ES 16 0001 - 91 ES 16 2260	2200
Carrera Cabriolet US and CDN	91 ES 17 0001 - 91 ES 17 1191	1131
Total for 1984		12888

Model year 1985 (F-Program)		
911 Model	Chassis number range	Production
Carrera Coupé	91 FS 10 0001 - 91 FS 10 3529	3469
Carrera Coupé Japan	91 FS 10 9501 - 91 FS 10 9722	162
Carrera Coupé US and CDN	91 FS 12 0001 - 91 FS 12 1959	1899
Carrera Targa	91 FS 14 0001 - 91 FS 14 1435	1375
Carrera Targa Japan	91 FS 14 9501 - 91 FS 14 9564	4
Carrera Cabriolet	91 FS 15 0001 - 91 FS 15 1583	1524
Carrera Cabriolet Japan	91 FS 15 9501 - 91 FS 15 9575	15
Carrera Targa US and CDN	91 FS 16 0001 - 91 FS 16 1942	1882
Carrera Cabriolet US and CDN	91 FS 17 0001 - 91 FS 17 1050	990
Total for 1985		11320

Model year 1986 (G-Program)		
911 Model	Chassis number range	Production
Carrera Coupé	91 GS 10 0001 - 91 GS 10 4031	3984
Carrera Coupé Japan	91 GS 10 9501 - 91 GS 10 9733	173
Carrera Coupé US and CDN	91 GS 12 0001 - 91 GS 12 2619	2559
Carrera Targa	91 GS 14 0001 - 91 GS 14 1758	1698
Carrera Targa Japan	91 GS 14 9501 - 91 GS 14 9579	8
Carrera Cabriolet	91 GS 15 0001 - 91 GS 15 2358	2300
Carrera Cabriolet Japan	91 GS 15 9501 - 91 GS 15 9580	20
Carrera Targa US and CDN	91 GS 16 0001 - 91 GS 16 1976	1916
Carrera Cabriolet US and CDN	91 GS 17 0001 - 91 GS 17 1986	1926
Total for 1986		14584

Model year 1987 (H-Program)		
911 Model	Chassis number range	Production
Carrera Coupé	91 HS 10 0001 - 91 HS 10 3381	3341
Carrera Coupé Japan	91 HS 10 9501 - 91 HS 10 9808	248
Carrera Coupé US and CDN	91 HS 12 0001 - 91 HS 12 2916	2856
Carrera Targa	91 HS 14 0001 - 91 HS 14 1354	1295
Carrera Targa Japan	91 HS 14 9501 - 91 HS 14 9579	19
Carrera Cabriolet	91 HS 15 0001 - 91 HS 15 1464	1407
Carrera Cabriolet Japan	91 HS 15 9501 - 91 HS 15 9585	25
Carrera Targa US and CDN	91 HS 16 0001 - 91 HS 16 2232	2172
Carrera Cabriolet US and CDN	91 HS 17 0001 - 91 HS 17 2653	2593
Total for 1987		13956

Model year 1988 (J-Program)		
911 Model	Chassis number range	Production
Carrera Coupé	91 JS 10 0001 - 91 JS 10 3580	3524
Carrera Coupé Japan	91 JS 10 9501 - 91 JS 10 9930	370
Carrera Coupé US and CDN	91 JS 12 0001 - 91 JS 12 2066	2066
Carrera Targa	91 JS 14 0001 - 91 JS 14 1281	1223
Carrera Targa Japan	91 JS 14 9501 - 91 JS 14 9580	20
Carrera Cabriolet	91 JS 15 0001 - 91 JS 15 1501	1444
Carrera Cabriolet Japan	91 JS 15 9501 - 91 JS 15 9581	21
Carrera Targa US and CDN	91 JS 16 0001 - 91 JS 16 1500	1440
Carrera Cabriolet US and CDN	91 JS 17 0001 - 91 JS 17 2116	2056
Total for 1988		12164

Model year 1989 (K-Program)		
911 Model	Chassis number range	Production
Carrera Coupé	91 KS 10 0001 - 91 KS 10 3532	3472
Carrera Coupé US and CDN	91 KS 12 0001 - 91 KS 12 1156	1096
Carrera Targa	91 KS 14 0001 - 91 KS 14 1063	1003
Carrera Cabriolet	91 KS 15 0001 - 91 KS 15 2787	1442
Carrera Targa US and CDN	91 KS 16 0001 - 91 KS 16 0860	800
Carrera Cabriolet US and CDN	91 KS 17 0001 - 91 KS 17 1361	1301
Total for 1989		9114

'Special' Production (1984 to 1989)			
911 Model	year	Description	Production
953 4x4	1984	91 ES 10 0020 - 91 ES 10 0022	3
Club Sport	1987	Row	81
	1988	Row	148
		USA	21
	1989	Row	83
		USA	7
Speedster	1989	Row: Turbo-Look	1124
		Row: Narrow Body	161
		USA & CDN: Turbo-Look	819
Total			2447

Total production number: 76473

No specific production figures are available for M491 Turbo-Look/Supersport.

Production numbers as supplied by Porsche AG.

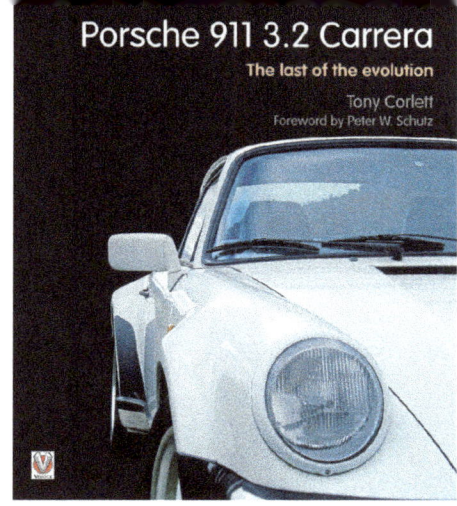

Chapter 18

Zuffenhausen - 1984 to 1989

In 1984, coinciding with the introduction of the new 911 Carrera, Porsche, despite being a family-owned company, offered non-voting preference shares on the stock exchange for the first time, and thus became Porsche Aktiengesellschaft (AG).

Dr Ing hc Ferry Porsche, son of the company's founder Dr Ing Ferdinand Porsche, had headed the company until 1972. Since then, a series of chairmen took over the reins, notably Professor Ernst Fuhrmann, who took over from Ferry Porsche and stayed until 1980. It was under his leadership that the 924, 944 and 928 cars were developed which, had he stayed in charge, would have seen the death of the 911 after the SC production run. After apparent disagreements with Ferry Porsche regarding the longevity of the 911, Fuhrmann resigned to make way for Peter W Schutz.

Very early in his leadership, Schutz met with Dr Helmuth Bott, the board member responsible for research and development, and, with a single stroke of his marker pen on Bott's production chart, Schutz indicated that 911 production would continue, much to the joy of Bott and his team at Porsche.

The 911 was resurrected, and the 3.2 Carrera was sanctioned to go ahead. This car had very nearly never made it to life, but for the intervention of Ferry Porsche and the then new Chairman Schutz. Schutz later said: "The Porsche 911, the company icon, had been saved, and I believe the company was saved with it".

By the mid-eighties, the number of Porsche employees had multiplied from a little over 1500 in 1965 to a little over 8000 in 1986. Correspondingly, the number of cars produced per year had increased from a little over 10,000 cars in 1965, to a little over of 50,000 cars in 1986. Porsche had undoubtedly come a long way in just twenty-one years, and this was largely due to the success of the 911.

The boardroom at Zuffenhausen in 1986 was filled by six men: Peter Schutz; his deputy, Heinz Branitzki, who subsequently took over as Chairman when Schutz retired in 1987; Professor Helmutt Bott was head of research and development; Kurt Femppel was head of personnel; Professor Rudi Noppen was head of production quality control; and Hans Halback was head of marketing.

Although Ferry Porsche had been, somewhat suprisingly, moved from the main factory by Schutz's predecessor Fuhrmann, Schutz chose to bring him back to the main headquarters, and kept him and the Porsche family close at hand in the business.

During the mid-eighties the Porsche company produced nine models: 924S, 944, 944S, 944 Turbo, 911 Carrera Coupé, 911 Targa, 911 Cabriolet, 911 Turbo and 928S4. The 911 and 928 ranges were built entirely at the Porsche factory at Zuffenhausen, while the 924 and 944 ranges were built in Neckarsulm.

For the 1985/86 financial year, the American market took the lion's share of Porsche cars. American exports claimed a huge 53.9 per cent of

An official 1986 Porsche photograph of an American specification Carrera Coupé with Sport Equipment. A 911 Carrera has over 6000 spot welds and more than 10 meters of seam welding.

production, ahead of Germany at 21.1 per cent, Great Britain at 7.2 per cent, France at 3.1 per cent, Switzerland at 2.9 per cent, Canada at 2.3 per cent. All other countries were at 9.5 per cent.

For the same period, the 944 range accounted for 48 per cent of total cars made, ahead of the 911 at 31.7 per cent, the 924 at 11.5 per cent, and the 928 at 8.8 per cent.

Research and development

Research and development played a big part in the success of Porsche cars. The Carrera was developed, as with all Porsche models, at Porsche's Weissach technical factory, where every element of a new or development model was researched, designed and developed into a production part. With facilities capable of producing full-size clay models, Weissach covered an extensive area of almost 50 hectares, which included 10 kilometres of road testing facilities. Weissach boasted 2200 employees, representing 30 per cent of the total Porsche staff, of which 1000 were engineers and 800 were specialists in prototype construction. A team of 45 filled the styling department and, with a full-size wind tunnel facility, Weissach represented a great base from which to launch the new 911 3.2 Carrera.

The Weissach R&D facility was started in the early nineteen-sixties and, by 1974, Porsche had moved all research and development there from Zuffenhausen. Weissach continued to expand through the nineteen-seventies and early nineteen-eighties to provide a state-of-the-art facility, not only for Porsche in the pursuit of 'Driving in its Purest Form', but also for outside contracts. Porsche claimed that something over 10 per cent of its annual costs was spent on research and development. During the nineteen-eighties, Weissach had seen investment of over DM1100 million, which included a full-scale wind tunnel, environmental test centre, a crash-test facility, and race-car test centre.

Crash testing was an important feature as Porsche developed the Carrera. Although earlier 911s still passed the then current legal crash-test requirements, the new facility introduced exacting records. Photographic records, taken at 1000 frames per second, allowed Porsche to individually monitor the level of adverse disturbance in a crash situation. Up to ten cameras would record the exact time of impact at 110 kilometres per hour, lasting no longer than one tenth of a second. The 911 Carrera was extremely rigid, and crash-test simulation only served to improve the already excellent design. Extra stiffening was introduced to the roof and door design to improve safety in side impact collisions.

To meet the tough American emissions controls, the Carrera was subjected to exhaustive testing in the new environmental test facility. Over two hundred technicians and engineers were available in this facility for continual testing and recording. These people were responsible for the development of Porsche's three-way catalytic exhaust system, fitted as standard to all US specification Carreras. Engine management was also under the control of the environmental facility where, with the aid of Bosch's Motronic injection system and Porsche's own data-fed

A Porsche promotional photograph of a 1989 Carrera Cabriolet.

E-Prom (Erasable Programmable Read Only Memory) microchip, the Carrera showed improved power with no increase of fuel consumption or emissions. The Carrera could be tested under simulated conditions of climate, altitude, and humidity, to satisfy emissions criteria for any given geographical location.

The introduction of the galvanised body in 1975 saw Porsche's Weissach facility all but combat rust in steel-bodied cars. In 1973, as part of Porsche's development programme, the engineers at Weissach hot-dip galvanised a 911, which they then left un-painted and exposed outside the factory in all weathers. This 911 was still in place during the nineteen-eighties without any degradation. With the introduction of new materials, Porsche suggested at the time that the expected lifespan of its cars was a minimum of twenty years, and one hundred and eighty thousand miles.

Prior to Weissach's new wind tunnel facility in 1986, all Porsche aerodynamic testing and development was undertaken at Stuttgart University. The Carrera's aerodynamic styling,

A Porsche promotional photograph of a 1984 Carrera Targa.

77

A Porsche promotional photograph of a 1988 Carrera Targa.

The Carrera Targa was a strong seller for Porsche throughout the world, offering the best of both the Coupé and Cabriolet.

The Targa, developed in 1965, retained as many of the Coupé production panels as possible to reduce tooling costs.

A Porsche promotional photograph of a 1988 Carrera Cabriolet.

including the development of the Sport Equipment front and rear spoilers, was carried out there. The Carrera, when tested in the Stuttgart University wind tunnel, was given a Cd value of 0.385.

Amongst the many diverse and interesting development programmes, Weissach developed a 3.2 flat-six based aircraft engine, the PFM 3200, which was due for production in 1987 but never made it.

In 1986, Porsche was building on average 30 911s per day, for which were between 70 and 100 customer options were available from the Porsche options list. Although Porsche offered 13 basic colour shades for the 911 Carrera, approximately every twentieth 911 was painted in a specific colour requested by the customer.

Approximately 500 sheet metal parts made up a 911 Carrera, all of either galvanised steel or aluminium. The build process of a 911 Carrera had approximately 6000 spot welds and approximately 10 meters of seam welding in each car which, together, made up 35 hours of production time.

The Carrera was manufactured almost entirely by hand; the newly installed robots were only used to feed and empty the machines for crankcase machining. Every spot weld, each stitch, and every drop of paint was carried out and/or applied by hand, by a technical workforce of the highest capability. This, in Porsche's opinion, was the vital feature of production. Porsche claimed that, along with quality, it was flexibility in the production process which hand work ensured. At the time, no technology matched the flexibility of a well-motivated Porsche production team.

Statistics at the time indicated that it was extremely rare to have two 911 Carreras built identically in any given month, such was the extent of the Porsche options and colour choices.

As part of the overall Porsche quality control, a computerised parts acceptance system was in place. This checked each and every part before it was made available to the production line. Massive importance was placed on quality by Porsche and, as a result,

the 3.2 Carrera was produced during a time when 'hand-made' was at its optimum. Parts were made to exacting standards and before the advent of robotised assembly; this car really was put together by engineers.

Mechanical components of the flat-six engine were machined by up to 200 specialist machine technicians. Machining was vital, and accounted for 15 per cent of the cost of the entire engine. The machined parts would then be taken to the engine department for final assembly. Although every engine technician was capable of building an entire engine on his own, in order to ensure continuity with all the engine ranges, each would work at 3 to 4 of the total 20 stations, switching between them every four weeks. This gave Porsche a great deal of versatility in its engine production which, at the time, was made up of 50 variations across the range.

As for the interior trim, each Carrera was individually produced using the best leather (or simulated leather and cloth), cut and stitched by hand. Banks

A Porsche promotional photograph of the 1987 Frankfurt Show Speedster.

of (mainly) women, all wearing a blue short-sleeved jacket type overalls with the distinctive Porsche logo on the pocket, fed thousands of yards of material through small industrial tabletop sewing machines. The body and engine production departments were staffed almost entirely by men, wearing green or grey dungarees with the Porsche logo across the front. Hard hats were worn during final assembly of body, engine and running gear.

Each Carrera was mounted on special cradle frames and painted as a whole car. The main body, front valance and bumper, boot lid, doors, engine cover, rear bumper, and skirts, were all located in the cradle for spraying together. The ancillary parts were positioned slightly away from the main body in order to allow paint to flow into concealed areas. After final quality checks and finishing, all edges were bound with protective tape and sent into the assembly area for trimming.

Final assembly of a Carrera required several thousand separate operations before every finished car was sent out for a 30 kilometre road test. Without exception, each Carrera was carefully tested by 40 experienced engineer drivers who checked the cars in the city, country and motorways, covering more than 40 control points. These engineer drivers were responsible for driving every Carrera manufactured with the aim of judging the behaviour of the car. Their feedback was critical in ensuring that the 911 Carrera was as driveable on the road as the technical statistics implied.

The finished Carreras were then sent to dispatch, for shipping to their ultimate destinations.

Randomly selected Carreras were also chosen from the production run for further testing on the test tracks and skid pans at Weissach. Handling tests were carried out on 40, 60 and 190 metre diameter skid pan circles. Each test was carefully monitored and recorded to test lateral 'g' force acceleration, braking 'g' forces, roll angles and steering forces.

On the 'paved and mountain track' at Weissach, the Carreras were tested for production faults relating to performance, acceleration, braking, handbrake operation, and fuel consumption. On the test track, the Carreras were checked for percentage speedometer and rev counter errors.

Long range testing of the Carrera included 16,000 kilometres at Weissach, incorporating the above, plus a further 80,000 kilometres, including 12,000 kilometres of town driving, 20,000 kilometres of country driving, 24,000 kilometres of *autobahn* driving, 6000 kilometres at the long Nürburgring track, and 18,000 kilometres at the Nardo track in Italy. Every element was carefully recorded and measured and compared to the predetermined 'expected' data.

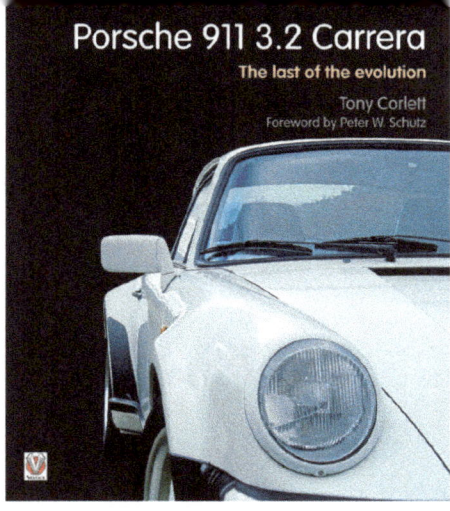

Chapter 19

Exterior aesthetics

The exterior of the Carrera was all about aesthetics. The shape, the stance, the luxurious paintwork, the panel fit; everything about the Porsche Carrera was sheer perfection.

There is no doubt that Porsche paintwork is amongst the best automotive finishes in the world, and the finish on the Carrera was no exception. The deep lustre of the paint finish showed off the sweeping lines of the 911 in the best possible way, and the first encounter with a Carrera left one with an extraordinary desire to experience more.

In design terms, the 911 shape could almost be described as two different cars moulded together.

The exterior quality of the Carrera was exacting in every respect. All body panels fitted with exceptional accuracy, and all opening panels functioned with perfect engineering precision.

Although the front is rather upright and stern, and the rear sweeping and relaxed, the two married together in a way that conveyed purpose and resolve.

As an overall package, the 911 Carrera was more practical than most sports cars. The very fact that it had a decent-sized boot, could seat two large adults and two children with relative comfort, and still notch up 150mph in a straight line really does speak volumes. Although relatively small in stature, the layout of the car provided the utmost use of space in a very matter-of-fact way.

Introduced to provide impact absorption for American legislation, the wraparound impact-bumper design was a strong feature of the 911 from 1974, the Carrera looking particularly imposing with them. Using rubber collapsible 'bellows', these impact-bumpers allowed the large cross-body member to move freely in the event of an accident.

Although Porsche provided 'federalised' engines to suit the American market, standing side by side, the bodies of European and American Carreras were virtually indistinguishable. The only identifying features of the American cars was the rear bumper, which was fitted with very much larger over-riders, the front indicator lenses, which incorporated a reflector and wrapped around to the bellows, and the red rear indicator lenses.

Blending the rather smoother body lines with the somewhat sturdier bumpers was carried out with great

Pages 82-84: Exterior detailing was carried out to perfection.

skill. Meeting the legal requirement to satisfy Porsche's largest single market, the integral and aesthetically-pleasing 'impact-bumper' solution was adopted on all Carreras. These colour-coded sectional bumpers comprised a large cross-body aluminium member, lower quarter panels, front and rear valance, a wraparound rubber bump-strip, side 'bellows', rubber over-riders to the rear bumper only, and a rubber connecting strip or 'smile' to the front. At the rear, the vertical lights and central reflector cross panel cluster sat snugly above the bumper, with wraparound indicator lenses meeting at the 'bellows' line. A single, large diameter exhaust pipe protruded from a cutout between the lower left quarter panel and the rear lower valance, and was angled for exit. At the front, indicator lenses were incorporated into the rubber bump-strip line, fog-light clusters were moulded into the lower valance, and a flat rubber strip, also affectionately known as the 'smile', was used to mask the gap between the cross-body bumper member and the leading edge of the bonnet.

Flowing up from the flat top surface of the front bumper and 'smile', the bonnet swept evenly up and widened out to the scuttle panel and lower windscreen. Two folds in the bonnet directed fresh air into the cabin air-intake grill. The intake grill was positioned directly below and centrally about the windscreen wiper pivots, and slightly inside the two windscreen washer jets. Everything was symmetrical and, apart from the windscreen wipers which rested towards the driver's side, for both left- and right-hand drive cars, the overall design was in complete balance.

The one piece front wings protruded forward and above the bonnet line, taking in the widening bonnet, front wheelarches and doors. On the left-hand wing, and set flush into the body line, was the fuel filler flap. This blended perfectly into the car's smooth lines, and was remotely operated, hinging forward to reveal

Impact bumpers move freely laterally without damage to the bodywork under light crash impact. The 'bellows' are designed to collapse and spring back to shape.

Later 1987 to 1989 Carreras incorporated the rear fog lamps into the reflector panel above the bumper. Carrera front light clusters were continued without change from the 911 SC, but incorporated two lower front driving lamps in the valance.

the fuel filler throat. The headlights sat upright, laying back only slightly.

The windscreen, too, was in perfect harmony with the rest of the front.

From the top edge of the rather stubby upright windscreen, a transformation occurred. The roof line swept over to the top of the very large and shallow-raked rear screen, then passed over the engine cowling to the top edge of the vertical light and cross panel cluster at the rear.

In profile, the Carrera's upper waist line ran almost horizontally, and added presence to the front end. This line ran along the top of the wing, below the side glass area, under the 'A' post, narrow 'B' post and sweeping 'C' post, with a definite downward sweep to the very corner of the rear light cluster. The 'C' posts flowed seamlessly into the rear wings, which in turn incorporated the flared rear wheelarches and flanks, stretching forward to the rear edge of the doors.

The shape of the doors echoed the design change from front to rear. The leading edge was vertical, whilst

A discreet 'Carrera' script logo was fitted on the engine cover. Cars were supplied without the logo under option M498 which was standard for the American market.

1984 to 1986 Porsche script rear reflector panel.

the rear edge was almost at a tangent to the sweeping roof line. The doors made up most of the car's flanks, and incorporated delicate sidescreen window frames with fixed quarter-lights. The mirrors were large and oblong, as opposed to sporting and rounded, yet somehow suited the overall bullish look of the Carrera.

The rear wheelarches were flared all round, whereas the front wheelarches had a smaller eyebrow design.

Most Sports Equipment cars, and all of the Supersport Equipment cars, were fitted with the robust Fuchs alloy wheels. Generally speaking, however, the standard cars had the more elegant Teledial alloys. The Carrera adopted a very purposeful stance on either design.

The finishing touches to the body were limited to practical accessories rather than flamboyant features. The door handles, side repeater indicators and screen wipers, front and rear, were

Quality did not stop at external looks.

all discreet and not overpowering. A black sill-line rubber stretched between the wheelarches and separated the lower flanks from the lower side-skirts. These lower skirts housed the manual jacking point which was also the balancing point or centre of gravity along the length of the car.

The door operation is like no other car; the distinctive and solid 'clunk' sound of a 911 door closing is instantly recognisable. The door handles were appropriate for such a gutsy car, and the squeeze lever handle operated with great precision, springing the door open cleanly and smoothly. The hinges, latches and strike plates worked together beautifully, and really made the first venture into 911 territory a pleasure. Shutting the doors required more than just a gentle nudge, more like a solid push actually, but once closed they fitted perfectly. The same was true of all the movable panels, which operated with precision and had perfect fit.

The engine cover and the bonnet lid were released via remote handles: a lockable pull release under the dashboard for the bonnet, and a simple lever within the left-hand door jamb for the engine cover.

In 1987, when the Carrera was updated, the external aesthetics remained largely unchanged (the windscreen washer jets were modified, and the rear light cluster was redesigned to incorporate fog lights). There was no longer any need for the lower rear fog lamp attachment, and the size of the Porsche logo script across the rear of the car was reduced.

A 16 inch diameter Fuchs alloy rear wheel as fitted to Sport equipped and Turbo-Look cars.

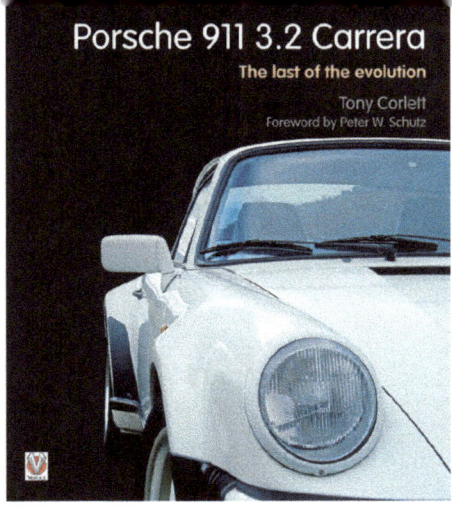

Chapter 20

Interior

The interior of the Carrera was, as you might expect of a German sports car, very functional, of high quality, and very well trimmed. Although entering a Carrera was easier than most low-slung sports cars, it still took a bit of practice, as getting your leading leg under the steering wheel was difficult and uncomfortable. A typical entry procedure would be as follows: lead leg in, bottom down, lead leg under the steering wheel, and then the other leg in.

Once in, the Recaro design sports seats did a great job of hugging the occupants. The front seats could slide backward and forward quite a long way, and could quite easily accommodate occupants of varying heights. Headroom was also very good. The same, however, could not be said of the rear seats, which comprised a small squab and back rest. Despite having more space than most sports cars, the rear seats were only adequate for small adults or children, and for shorter trips.

The rear seat rests could be hinged forward and laid flat, forming a luggage shelf (once again, showing that practicality was an important consideration for the designers). The earlier cars had a leather strap and popper to hold the seat-back in the upright position, clipping to the rear parcel shelf, whereas later cars had a mechanical pin at the hinge point which did the same job.

An interesting link between Porsche and Recaro is worthy of note. In 1963, Reutter Carzozzerie Coachbuilders sold its body company to Porsche K.G. so that, in 1964, the bodies would be built by Karmann and Porsche. The Reutter family continued to build the seats, under the company name 'Recaro', which was a combination of 'Reutter' and 'Carzozzerie'.

The trim was of exceptional quality and finish. Basically two upholstery specifications were offered with the Carrera: standard cloth, or full leather. The standard finish had soft cloth pinstripe design inserts in the centre of the front seats, the door panels and the rear seats. As fitted as standard to the 911 Turbo, or as an option on the Carrera, the full leather finish included the front seats and door panels, with matching leather or leatherette for the rear seats. With both trims, the rear parcel shelf, dashboard, fascia and door tops were finished in a matching leatherette. A great many trim variations were offered on the Carrera, including full leather for some or all of the above, and colour contrasting 'piping' to the front seats.

Expertly manufactured, the luxurious thick woollen pile carpets were generally loose fitting, with all exposed edges trimmed with leatherette to match the colour of the carpet or optional seat 'piping'. The backs of the fold-down rear seats were also trimmed with carpet, which meant that the parcel shelf was in keeping with the finish when folded flat.

The cabin headlining was leatherette, as were the two sun visor covers, each fitted with a vanity mirror.

The dashboard and fascia were neat and functional. A soft, leatherette or optional leather, roll-top dashboard cushion extended across the top of the

Although the basic 911 interior format was adopted for the 1984 Carrera, a number of modifications and luxury additions were made to later cars.

A 1984 Coupé with half-leather seats and pinstripe cloth inserts. There were smaller fresh air vents on earlier Carreras.

Rear seats had a seat base and independent seat-back which hinged forward to provide a flat luggage area.

fascia, around the top of the instrument binnacle, and rolled over to meet the simple black fascia. Immediately in front of the driver was the instrument binnacle, housing five instrument gauges. In the centre of the dashboard, within the roll-top cushion, were the fresh air vents, below which were a group of three switches and three warning lights. Below these was the radio/tape audio equipment. The glove box was on one side of the radio, and the ventilation controls were on the other. There were fresh air ventilation outlets at eacch end of the black fascia, and along the lower edge of the black fascia was a leatherette or optional leather trimmed bump-strip, with a centrally-positioned ashtray.

The dashboard and fascia layout on right-hand drive cars was essentially a mirror image of that on left-hand cars, with the exception of the instrument binnacle, glove box lid, and the petrol flap pull release.

There were some subtle changes to the dashboard and fascia of later 1987 to 1989 Carreras. These included substantially larger ventilation outlets, and a relocated internal temperature thermostat.

A variety of controls and switches were located on the fascia panel and in and around the instrument binnacle. On the fascia were the ignition switch, headlight switch, hazard light switch, ventilation controls, radio/tape player, rear window demister switch, fog light switch, cigarette lighter, glove box, and warning lights for seatbelts, handbrake and brake pad wear. Located within and under the instrument binnacle fascia were the rear screen wiper switch (when fitted), the headlight washer switch, the intermittent flick wipe rheostat switch, the sunroof switch (when fitted), and the left/right door mirror switch (when fitted).

The ventilation sliders operated dampers behind the dashboard, directing hot or cold air to various outlets for driver comfort and window demisting.

In front of the gear lever, on the floor in the centre of the car, was a small utility/console unit which provided space for audio cassettes

A 1986 Cabriolet with roof folded.

A 1988 Coupé with full leather interior, larger air vents and a leather gear stick surround.

1984 Coupé with full leather interior.

Rear seat-backs fixed in upright position. Early Carreras had a leather tag and popper-clip to hold them back against the rear shelf.

Rear seat-backs laid down to form a luggage shelf. Later Carreras had a mechanical fixing at the pivot.

Door lock thumb-turn in leather door trim.

and switches for audio speaker control and air-conditioning (when fitted). The gear lever itself was quite basic; a tall slender tube bent over slightly at the top, with a neat bulb handgrip, running down into a small rubber boot at the bottom. Later cars had a leatherette, or optional leather wrap. Behind the gear lever, between the seats, was the handbrake lever.

The main hot air control switch was positioned between the seats, behind the handbrake lever. A circular switch, with ten individual cold to hot settings, controlled the hot air coming into the cabin from the heat exchangers on the underside of the engine. The older, SC dual levers were used for the lighter Club Sport and Speedster, one each for the driver and passenger.

An option on the Carrera (standard on the 911 Turbo) the fully-automatic air-conditioning system offered combined heating, ventilation and cooling, maintaining a pre-selected temperature.

The dashboard binnacle carried a five-dial display. In the centre, and directly in front of the driver, was the large, and somewhat legendary, circular 911 tachometer. To either side of the tachometer was the speedometer and the oil-pressure/temperature gauges. To either side of these were the clock and the fuel/temperature dials.

The steering wheel came in two designs: the earlier, three-spoke design had the Stuttgart crest motif in the centre, whereas the later four-spoke 'sport' design featured the Porsche script logo. There were two levers mounted on the steering column, one to either side. The left-hand lever controlled the indicators and headlight dip and main beam,

In celebration of the 25th year of the 911 and the 250,000th 911 to roll of the production line, the 1988 Carrera was available with special 'Celebration' livery, including Diamond Blue metallic paintwork and matching interior leather. An image of Ferry Porsche's signature was incorporated into the front seats.

As part of the weight saving package, the Club Sport did not have the rear seats fitted, nor the rear side trim panels and rear parcel shelf.

the right-hand lever controlled the windscreen wiper functions and the windscreen washers.

The sunroof (when fitted), the door mirrors, the front windows and, in most later cars, the front seats, were all electrically-operated. A Blaupunkt radio/tape player was fitted as standard, and output was through four audio speakers, two on the back shelf and one in each door. The front seatbelts were inertia-reel items, whereas the rear were lap belts.

The way the doors operated demonstrated the overall high quality of the 911 Carrera. The vertical locking button, which closed flush and couldn't be lifted, was fitted on top of the door, immediately behind the quarter-light. Directly below the button was a recessed knurled wheel that, when turned, forced the button back up, thus unlocking the door. The door release handle was incorporated within an armrest/door pull handle, which also contained a flip-top storage bin.

The windows were electrically-powered, except on the Club Sport and Speedster which had manual window winders. The electric window winder switches were mounted on the doors, the driver's door carrying switches for both windows.

Internal storage was by way of the lockable glove locker, and 'bins' on each door. The Speedster also had two lockable compartments below the rear shelf.

Everything operated in a very positive and reassuring manner. The interior of the Carrera was as well engineered as the rest of the car, and using the controls was a delight. Comfort was good, visibility was good, and the driving position was good.

The Carrera's luggage compartment was located between the front wings, above the fuel tank and spare wheel well. It was fully carpeted and remarkably large, and got progressively wider towards the windscreen. Luggage needed to be carefully chosen, however, but the space was not as restrictive as it might seem at first. The carpet for the boot lining comprised four basic mats, all moulded to fit around the floor, two wings and rear scuttle cover. An option of upgrading the carpet from the standard tight weave, to the luxurious wool as used within the passenger cabin, was offered.

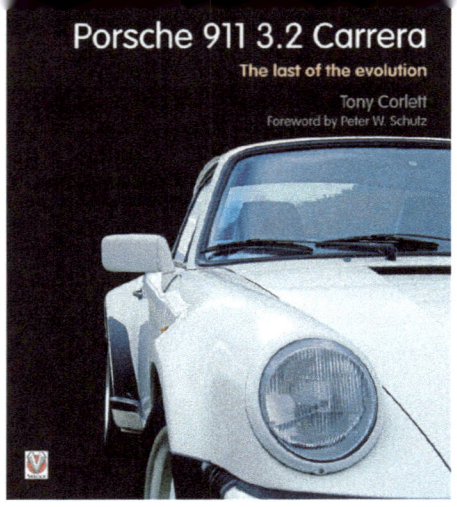

Chapter 21

Attention to detail

The overall quality of the Carrera was evident in the detailing. The best engineers in the world designed and built this car, and every aspect was carefully engineered and designed to give maximum operational capability, longevity and aesthetics. From the operation of the control switches, to the neatness of the moulded fuel cell, nothing about the Carrera was left to chance.

To underline Porsche's dedication to quality, Prof Dr ing Rudi Noppen, the then board member responsible for Production, Quality Control and Supply Economics, said: "A high quality level is the primary goal in the actual production process. When business is good, manufacturers are easily tempted to raise production numbers at the expense of quality. This is not our way - quality quite obviously takes priority".

Technically, every Porsche benefited from the team of development engineers at Weissach. With regard to Weissach, Prof. Helmuth Bott, the then board member responsible for Research and Development said: "Our main task is to develop new products for our own company and to maintain our production cars at a high technical level".

A staunch dedication to achieving perfection drove both the development and production lines, which worked hand in hand to achieve an exceptional standard of quality for every car produced. Customers came to expect this level of quality, and Porsche excelled in meeting its customers' expectations.

The then Chairman Peter W Schutz said: "The synthesis of common taste with individual demands is the basis for close ties between all Porsche drivers". And he was right. It's not just for the elite few, but rather a quality that permeates through each and every Porsche ever made. And it all boils down to one simple phenomenon - attention to detail. Once this is understood and entrenched, anything is possible. Porsche cars are proof of that.

Porsche's attention to detail was second to none.

An engineering and production quality driven policy ensured that every Carrera manufactured was of the highest possible standard in every respect.

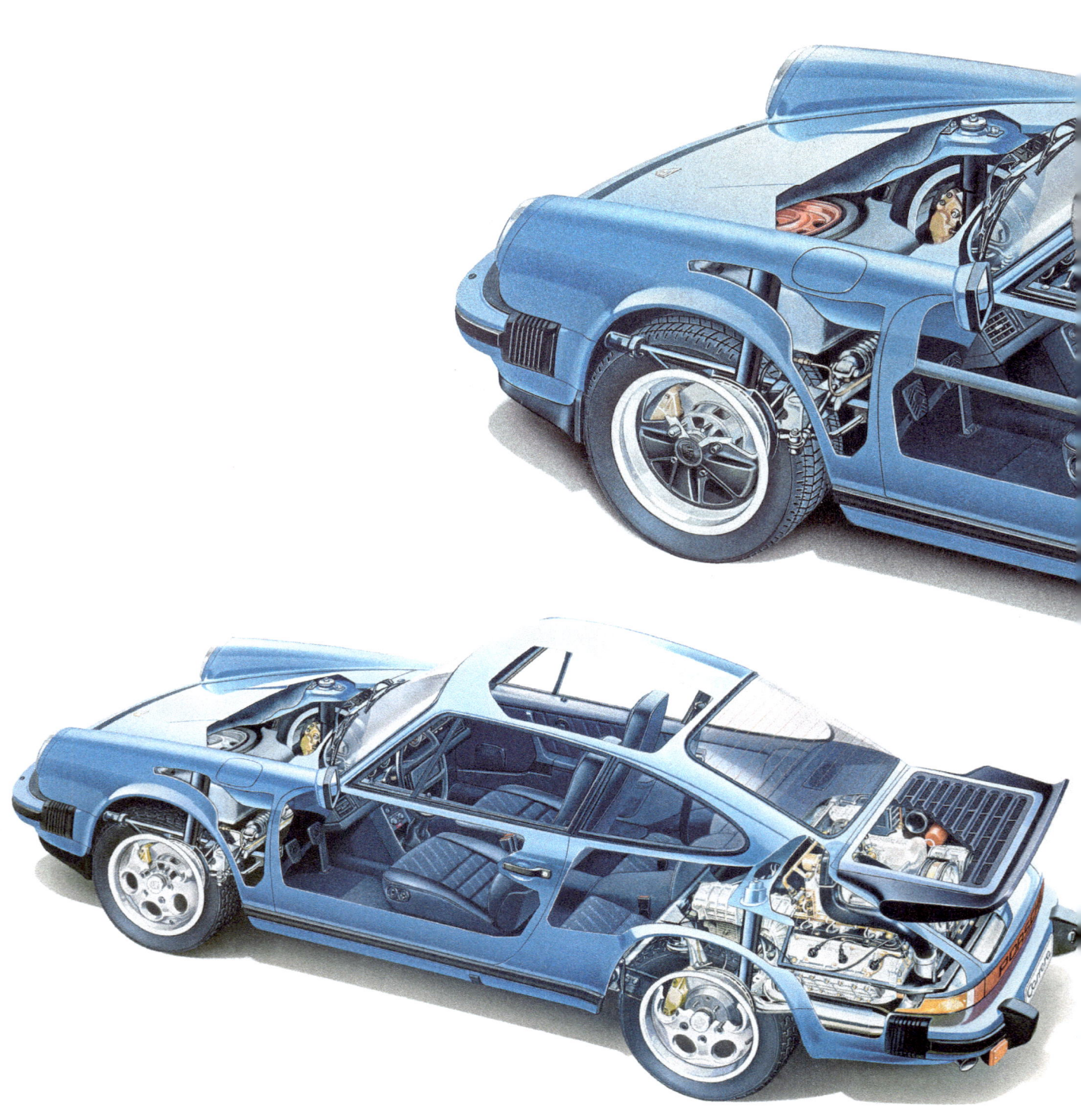

Official Porsche cut-away drawing shows both earlier 915 (left) and later G50 (above) gearbox-equipped cars. Differences include wheels, gearbox and side impact protection bars. Note the chassis changes behind the rear seat for the different gearboxes.

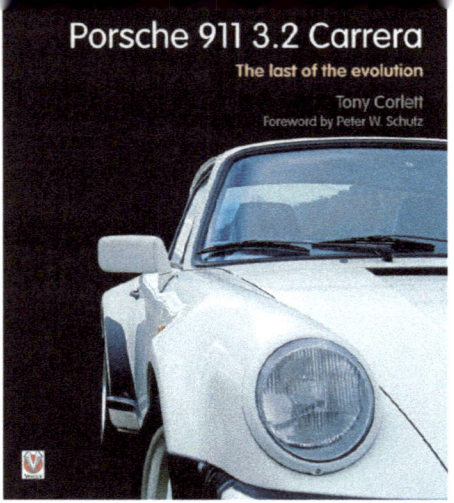

Chapter 22

At the controls

The 911 Carrera is a very comfortable car. The driver's seat, the steering wheel, the gear lever, and the pedal positions are extremely well situated, and inspire the sort of confidence that comes from being properly in command of the controls.

As with the windscreen, the steering wheel is quite steeply raked. This reinforces the sense of sitting up, as opposed to laying back, and improves visibility to the four corners of the car. Gear changes are comfortable, as is the steering, though this can be heavy when the wide Sport Equipment tyres are fitted.

The classic 911 dashboard layout is very evident in the Carrera. The large diameter, centrally-mounted tachometer, and the four flanking dials, give the impression that this is a place to conduct the business of driving fast. The tachometer, which dominates the driver's view of the information array, was drawn straight from the world of racing.

There are two steering column-mounted levers. The indicators and the headlight dip and main beam lever is on the left, the windscreen wiper and windscreen washer lever is on the right. Both are at finger length, are very comfortable to use, and operate very firmly and precisely.

The accelerator, brake and clutch pedals are floor-mounted and can take a bit of getting used to. The operation is, however, very positive, and the clutch is not heavy. The position of the brake in relation to the accelerator does not easily allow for heel and toe down shifts, which is a shame. The gear lever is functional and stands high from a low centre console, and the handbrake lever rests between the seats and is easily operated.

Right-hand drive Carreras have a pedal-box offset. The pedals are closer to the centre of the car than of those on the left-hand drive cars. This can take a little time to get used to, with the brake pedal being where the clutch pedal would ordinarily be.

Glass area is relatively large, visibility is good, and there are no major blind spots. It has to be said that the 911 Carrera is exceptionally relaxing as sports cars go, and really does inspire confidence in the driver. The view behind is also good, both door mirrors and the rear view mirror offering good visibility for rear view observation and reversing.

The typical 911 dashboard layout was carried forward for use in the Carrera. The display is dominated by the large centrally-mounted rev counter. This is a 1984 Coupé with a three-spoke steering wheel.

1988 Coupé with four-spoke steering wheel.

1989 Club Sport with four-spoke steering wheel fitted as standard.

Official factory photograph of a 1984 dashboard with four-spoke leather steering wheel.

Right-hand drive Speedster dashboard showing the typical layout of later Carreras. Note the manual door window winder as fitted to the Speedster and Club Sport.

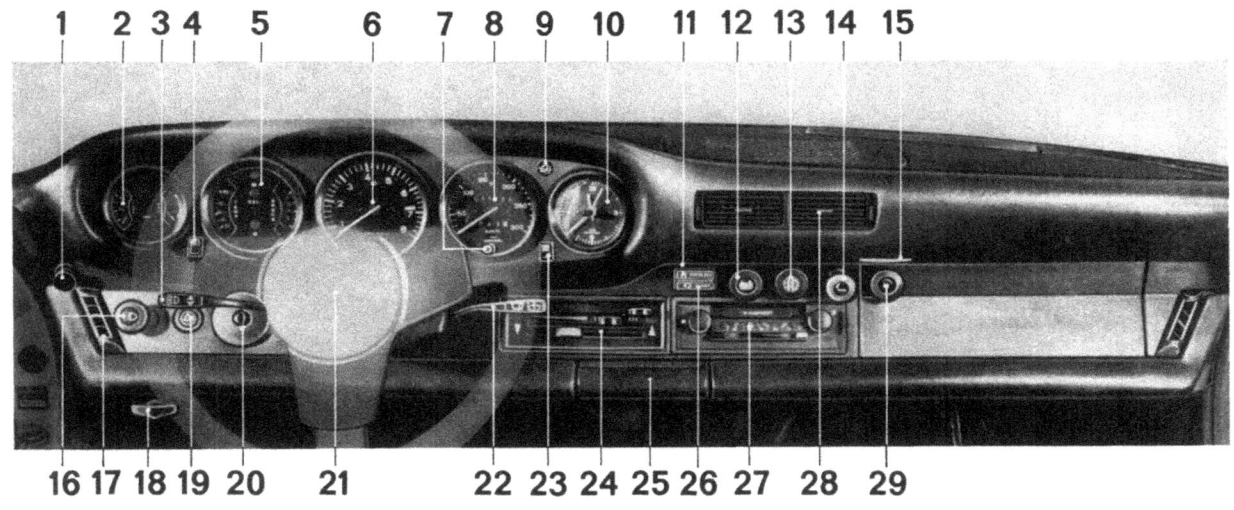

The standard layout of a 1984 dashboard and controls as shown in the Porsche handbook:

1. Fuel flap release pull.
2. Small combination instrument dial.
3. Indicator stalk.
4. Rear screen wiper switch.
5. Large combination instrument dial.
6. Tachometer.
7. Odometer trip button.
8. Speedometer.
9. Intermittent windscreen wiper timer switch.
10. Clock.
11. Seatbelt indicator light.
12. Heated rear window switch.
13. Front and rear fog lamp switch.
14. Cigarette lighter.
15. Map light.
16. Light switch.
17. Fresh air intake vent.
18. Luggage compartment release knob.
19. Hazard lights button.
20. Ignition switch.
21. Steering wheel.
22. Windscreen wiper stalk.
23. Headlamp washer switch.
24. Heater and ventilation slide controls.
25. Ashtray.
26. Brake warning lights.
27. Audio player.
28. Fresh air inlet vents.
29. Glove locker.

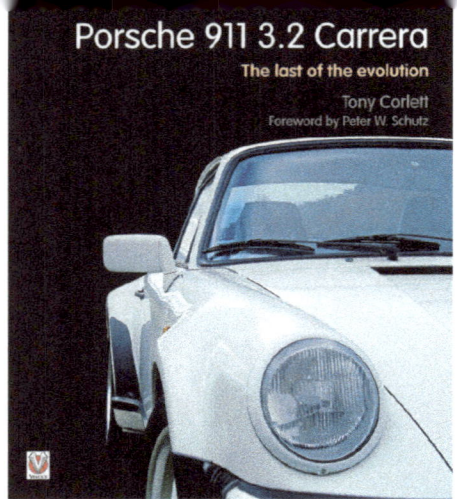

Chapter 23

Driving impressions

For a good driver, a well set up 911 Carrera is a joy to drive. A poor driver, on the other hand, may never get near the car's limits (which is probably just as well) but will certainly have a lot of fun. I believe that the 911's reputation for being 'tail-happy' has a lot to do with the poor quality of the drivers who 'think' they can drive fast, and inevitably end up in trouble.

For everyday use, and compared to other, more brutish sports cars, the 911 Carrera is actually quite easy to drive. For most drivers, the 911 Carrera will go where it is pointed (up to a point) and accelerate more than adequately. However, things get a little more complicated when driving a 911 quickly turns into driving it fast. That's when all the car's adverse idiosyncrasies start to manifest themselves.

The key to driving a 911 Carrera fast (and safely) is knowing about and understanding the car's characteristics. For example, the two basic 'rules' for driving a 911 are: never lift off the

Official 1987 Porsche photograph of a Club Sport undergoing road tests.

On the road, the Carrera is a very confidence building sports car to drive fast. Handling is precise and power delivery is strong all the way to the red line.

throttle in a corner, and; don't turn-in under braking. It's a learned 911 driver who gets away with breaking either of these rules.

The engine is the heaviest object in any car, and it's usually mounted within or over the axle lines. For the 911 Carrera, however, the engine was mounted in an 'outboard' position, behind the rear axle line. This is fine in normal circumstances but, when cornering, gravitational forces can cause a pendulum effect and spin the car. The 911 will actually spin about its front wheels, which would effectively be the fulcrum point of the pendulum.

As the 911 was developed to deliver more power, the suspension, roadholding and handling were also improved. The earlier, 'loose' handling car gradually evolved into something that stuck like glue until the moment it reached maximum gravitational pull (whereupon it would let go in one giant swing, rather than a gentle and controllable slide). Because the maximum gravitational pull point is extremely high, 0.85g, once reached, there is very little that can be done to prevent the car from letting go.

Driving a Carrera on the limit really does require total commitment. It takes a thorough understanding of how a 911 behaves to really appreciate how it handles. The feeling of holding a Carrera under control as the rear end lightens up under hard braking is fabulous.

Under normal driving conditions, understeer - where the front end washes away during cornering, and is rectified only by controlled power-off

- is the Carrera's worst characteristic. Understeer is, however, built into the handling of the Carrera, and is there to provide a safety margin for the average driver. With understeer built in, and under normal road use, the heavy tail would first have to overcome the front of the car before spinning around. For example, if you arrive at a corner too quickly, turning-in will result in understeer, and most drivers would lift off the throttle (normally a mistake). However, provided the car is still under control, lift-off oversteer will counteract the understeer. Without the built in understeer, the tail would come round under exactly the same cornering situation.

Although a skilled driver may be able to trail the brake pedal when cornering, and even brake quite hard into corners, it's generally best to brake in a straight line to prevent the tail coming round. Although the understeer will provide some degree of safety against unavoidable late braking, if you get it all wrong, the Carrera will oversteer and spin, and there's very little you can do about it. Don't let that put you off, though; the Carrera's limits are a long way off and, provided you keep things tidy, you'll not run into trouble.

With the exception of the most severe oversteer conditions, you should never attempt to correct oversteer

With a 40/60 front to rear weight distribution, the Carrera has excellent traction under acceleration.

oversight on the part of the Porsche engineers or, more likely, a way of preventing both pedals being depressed at the same time.

The gear changes on the earlier type 915 gearboxes, as fitted during 1984, 1985 and 1986, are rather long, and can be a little cumbersome. However, the later type G50 gearbox, as fitted during 1987, 1988 and 1989, has a shorter throw and better selection which make gear changes a little more comfortable. The purists will argue that the Porsche type 915 gearbox is more true to the 911 package, and, therefore, should be more rugged and tough in keeping with the rest of the car. Although I have a lot of sympathy with that, the Getrag type G50 is slick and does select a lot more positively, making the later G50 cars a little easier on the driver.

For normal day to day driving, the 911 Carrera is one of the easiest sports cars to drive. You can see most of the front end, it provides good all round visibility, and the driving position is such that you sit up, as opposed to slumping down. The steering wheel is very vertical, and reach is not compromised by the pedal positions. The 911 Carrera is an all-round comfortable car, which makes it all the better for confident driving.

using the steering wheel. Instead, stay on the throttle, and ride it out, letting the natural understeer do its job. The feeling of controlling a rampant Carrera is second to none. When you reach this stage of total commitment, you'll experience the real beauty of a 911 chassis and walk away with a grin.

The Carrera brake and accelerator pedals are not positioned for heel and toe driving as the the brake pedal is much higher. This was either an

The Carrera is subject to traditional rules for driving a 911. Under normal road driving conditions, brake in a straight line and don't lift off the throttle in a bend.

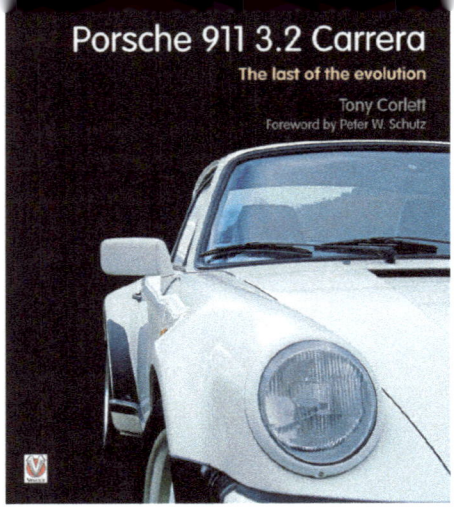

Chapter 24

On the Track

Driving a Carrera on a race track is probably the best driving experience you'll ever have behind the wheel of a 911.

In the dry
The first thing you'll notice, which is far more pronounced on a circuit than on a road, is the understeer. This is most evident on fast sweeping corners. Lifting-off the throttle is required to induce oversteer to tame the lateral pull, but this will compromise your lap time, of course. You can modify the suspension settings and stiffness to overcome cornering understeer, but I'm primarily discussing standard Carrera specifications here.

It can be quite hard work keeping a rampant 911 Carrera on the limit. The lightening up of the tail, it has to be said, is a major feature of the overall experience and can be a little tricky under braking, particularly if you like to trail the brake pedal or simply brake under turn-in.

Understeer is the Carrera's biggest handling trait, and no more so than on the circuit where long fast curves will require lift-off oversteer.

Club Sports are used regularly on circuits around the world. Here is a typical example at Leguna Seca in America.

In the hands of the experienced, wet track driving can produce some of the Carrera's finest moments.

Club Sports compete all over the world. This is a UK specification Carrera in Australia.

That's what it's all about, however, the feeling of taking the car to the limit, but remaining squarely in control. You'll know when you get there, as you will be hard on the brake, turning the car in and balancing the tail on the steering, probably locking up the inside front, the rear just begging to lead the way.

A Carrera will only take so much sideways motion before it goes completely, however, and when that happens, it happens fast, usually allowing no time to gather it all up. But then that's what you're on the circuit for, to find the cars limits and to enjoy this wonderful chassis and power balance.

A Carrera will deliver its power right up to the red line. The trick is to change up just before the inbuilt Bosch rev limiter spoils the fun. Typical track gears would be third, fourth and fifth (depending upon the length of the straight) which will provide good acceleration. Keeping the tachometer needle above 4000rpm is the objective here, but the torque range is so good in this car that it will catapult forward from just about any rev.

The track braking capacity of a standard Carrera is good. Compared to more modern cars, however, particularly with larger callipers, it's quite a task to get the braking points right. Obviously, as you learn, you can brake later and later into a corner, trailing the pedal with turn-in, but you'll reach the limit sooner or later.

At something like 125mph in fourth gear, a braking distance of at least 100 meters would be required for a fast third gear bend. Compare this with a lighter, more nimble race or track car and you'll find the Carrera needs twice as much for braking.

The pedal will remain quite firm, but brake fade will start to creep in as the standard, original equipment discs and pads start to glaze and the brake fluid gets hotter. Eventually, you'll run out of good pressure after several laps at hard speeds, but, generally, the pedal will stay quite confident if you ease back for a lap or two and let things cool down.

The steering is very responsive and provides a very good feel to the front of the car. Initial turn-in is strong and can lead to a false sense of security later in a longer sweeping bend as the understeer takes over.

Body roll is actually quite extensive on a Carrera and it can drag the car off line if you get a little over-enthusiastic. With uprated torsion bars and harder dampers it is possible to reduce this, but the overall sharpness of turn-in is inherent within the chassis.

The rear outside tyre, as you might expect, takes most of the load on 911 circuit driving. It is important to keep an eye on the temperatures of the rear tyres, especially on normal roadgoing tyres, and to ensure they are not wearing too harshly.

Generally speaking, the 911 Carrera is an easy car to drive quickly on a circuit, although it does get harder the more you push it. I guess that's the same with any track car, the Carrera is just that little more anarchic. There is no substitute for track driving and track experience. Anyone who really wants to experience a 911 would be well advised to take it to a track and play. You'll be amazed at just how fast a Carrera can be around a circuit, and, where it loses out over lighter cars, on overall cornering speed, braking, grip and acceleration, the straight line grunt will make up for it.

Kinks and chicanes probably offer the most exhilarating part of track driving a Carrera; the ability to brake right into the turn, turning-in towards the first apex, then using the car's pendulum effect to set it up for the next apex, in effect, catching a 911 out at its own game. The switch in direction can really be sharp, allowing full power through and out of the second apex. For a chicane, it's just a matter of doing this twice, dumping the car into the third apex quite harshly, again using the pendulum pull to great effect. Manhandle the car and it seems to know who's boss under these conditions and simply hangs on, despite all the feelings to the contrary. You're dumping all the weight to the

The best way to experience a Carrera is on the track.

Part of the joy of experiencing a 911 Carrera on the circuit is to firstly understand how it reacts under pressure.

outside wheels and turning into the slide, but that's exactly where you want to go. You've caught it out again.

Things are relatively predictable in the dry, of course, but add a slip-plane and a measure of adverse weather, and things get much more complicated.

IN THE WET

I've always been a lover of wet driving; in fact, the wetter the better. It's the only way to really challenge the limits of car and driver. Different lines, sometimes odd braking and turn-in points, and cautious throttling and braking make wet track driving quite exhilarating.

Braking and acceleration have to be carefully balanced with steering control. You're on the limit when you find the right balance, and finding the Carrera's 'sweet-spot' in the wet is sometimes better than dry and sticky racing.

Some people shy away from driving a 911 in the wet, which is definitely a shame (some of my finest moments have been in the wet, and as for the spray off the rear wing, well that's just fantastic).

On a wet track, all your actions, both in the cockpit and on the track surface, must be gentle. If you can avoid harsh and sharp movements you'll be fine. A light shower after a warm period will make the circuit very slippery and sometimes impossible to read. Get a good downpour, however, and the grip comes back, that's if you know where to find it and how to handle it.

Take a few laps to understand the track surface. The first few laps will feel greasy and generally unpleasant, but as you begin to find grip and feel the car's attitude, you'll get quicker.

I particularly remember one wet track day, where, after some heavy rain, some grip had returned. Through standing water, continual rain and spray, I was spinning the rear wheels on the straight in fourth, my focus firmly fixed on the two red spots visible through the spray in front. It was fellow Carrera owner Mike Chadwick, this time

Body roll in a standard Carrera is quite severe under hard cornering. Some detailed modifications to the suspension set up will reduce this for regular circuit use.

out in his Caterham Road Sport. Usually a good few seconds quicker than me in the dry, here I was slowly reeling him in. I had found the sweet-spot, was braking early, running wide looking for grip, and powering on without upsetting the rear end; my Carrera was buzzing. My Dunlop Sport tyres, with very scrubbed (just how I like them for dry sessions) were far from ideal for shifting the water, but never once compromised the enjoyment.

After several fast and demanding laps, and with the Caterham almost within my grasp, I missed my early brake point into the sharp right-hander at the end of the main straight. I ran into the standing water too fast, locked up, missed the apex, ran way too wide, just missed a few cones, and those red lights were a distant blur again. I pitted a few laps later, sweat pouring from me such was my concentration. Such experiences really bring the joys of a 911 Carrera to the fore, and the memories never fade.

If you do a lot of track drives, a number of simple modifications will make a difference. One is to have a strut brace fitted to the tops of the front turrets, and another is to replace the standard Porsche brake pads with a set that will handle and disperse the heat more efficiently. Other good ideas include using a brake fluid with better viscosity at high temperatures, and fitting tyres with a compound that works better at hotter temperatures, perhaps even go for a semi-slick road tyre. Naturally, the stiffer the suspension the better, but that involves major work and might not necessarily suit your road driving conditions.

Whatever you do in a Carrera, the car needs to be set up correctly in the first place. Spend time on that and you'll never look back: you're never going to find buckets more power, the standard engine is good to start with, so enjoy what the Porsche engineers spent a lot of time and effort perfecting.

A change of torsion bars, anti-roll bars, and dampers can eliminate body roll.

A well set up Carrera will be a thrill to drive in the wet.

911 Carrera

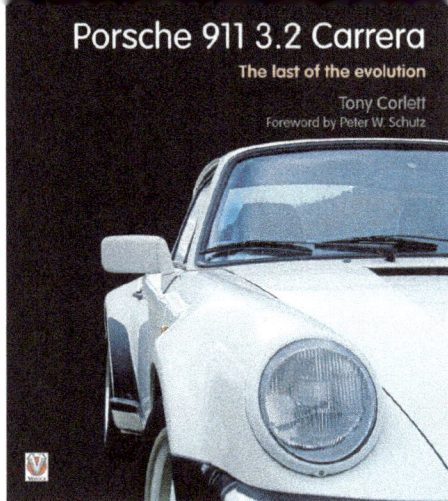

CHAPTER 25

953 4X4 PARIS TO DAKAR

The toughest race of them all ... survival of the fittest, not necessarily the fastest, but the Paris to Dakar Rally is a tough nut to crack. Jacky Ickx was determined to match his 1983 rally victory, this time with his own development programme Porsche 911 Carrera.

In 1983, Ickx and a Porsche development crew spent two months in Algiers trying and testing the new and radical Porsche four-wheel-drive system in the desert. It was an ambitious project and Ickx was confident that the 3.2-litre four-wheel-drive 911 would conquer the tough conditions of Africa.

Linked with Rothmans tobacco sponsorship from the Porsche track endurance cars, and under the team management of Porsche's head of race sport development, Peter Falk, Porsche officially entered three identical 911 Carreras, code named 953, in the 1984 Paris - Dakar Rally, with backup coming in the form of an entire racing crew with large service vehicles.

In Paris, Jacky Ickx said " ... it's an off-road rally; most of the tracks we are using are used sometimes only two or three times a year, so there are really no roads. You have to be so careful and you have to be so aware of the problems of the road itself, so the tension during the rally is very high. As you know, we have to race between six and nine hours a day, on off-road racing, with a four-wheel-drive car ..."

And about the car he said " ... it is a Porsche 911, it looks like a Porsche but it has four-wheel-drive and it's prepared for the desert and off-road racing, so it means the ground clearance is very high, it's nearly thirty centimetres. It has a 3.2-litre engine, and it has 330bhp ..."

The three 911 Carreras, built using 1984 'E' program 911 chassis, were WPOZZZ91ZES100020 (car 175), WPOZZZ91ZES100021 (car 176) and WPOZZZ91ZES100022 (car 177). Car 175 was driven by world endurance champion and ex-formula one driver Jacky Ickx, partnered by French film star Claude Brasseur. Car 176 was driven by 1981 rally winner and French saloon car champion Rene Metge, partnered by Dominique Lemoyne. Car 177, the team chase-car car, was driven

Under the leadership of Porsche works driver Jacky Ickx, Porsche engineered three four-wheel-drive 911 Carreras to successfully tackle the 1984 Paris to Dakar Rally.

Ickx at speed in the desert.

Service area.

Kussmaul at speed in the desert.

Rally winner Rene Metge in car number 176.

Kussmaul tackling a river crossing.

The winning car at rest on the beach at Dakar.

by Porsche factory engineers Roland Kussmaul and Erich Lerner.

The 953 variant, derived from the SC RS (954), used a stock, flat-six 3.2 Carrera engine producing over 300bhp. This car was effectively an all-wheel-drive version of the 911 SC RS, which later provided the platform for the 959 four-wheel-drive system. The 953 used a manually-operated four-wheel-drive system, the driver being able to operate the drive wheels using a series of levers. This was superseded in the 959 with a variable torque split function.

The race was dominated by the Porsches, with a clear victory for Metge in car number 176, Ickx bringing his 911 home in sixth place, having had by far the majority of the failures and bad luck of the three. The chase-car of Roland Kussmaul came home in 26th place, having suffered two rolls and a few lengthy time delays in performing his team duties of helping the two other 911s.

The 953 Carrera 4x4 has, to some extent, missed out on Porsche racing history (the 1984 Paris to Dakar Rally being its only competition). It may be the case that it was only ever regarded as a development tool for the 959.

911 Carrera

Official Porsche publicity poster following the 1984 Paris to Dakar win. "Rally Paris-Dakar '84: A victory for Porsche technology and reliability".

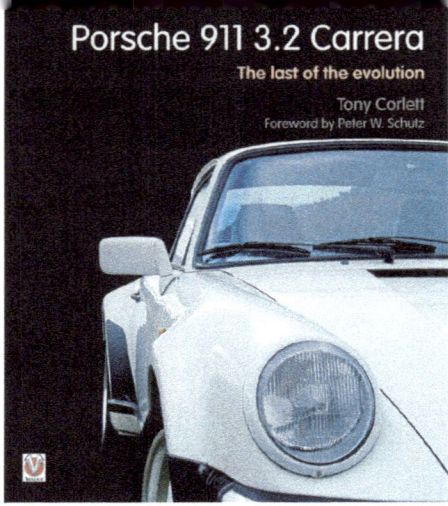

Chapter 26

CTR Yellow Bird

Group C Turbo Ruf (CTR)

It was extremely unlikely that Porsche could ever have built this 911, because it went against the company's mission statement of providing "prudent and refined" sports cars. It could be argued that Porsche *should* have built this car, but it chose to develop the 959, with its all-wheel-drive system and somewhat 'comprehensive' specification, instead.

For a small private engineering concern which could throw caution to the wind and ignore the rulebook, however, taking a 911 to the absolute limits of everything known to man at the time was an indulgence just waiting to happen.

The technically advanced 450bhp 959 Group B-based 911, developed under the control of Helmuth Bott, was first shown by Porsche in 1983, and went into limited production in 1987. In the same year, Ruf introduced the 469bhp CTR based on a standard Carrera chassis and body (though that's where the similarity ends). Whereas Porsche used a mallet to accurately crack the nut, Ruf used a sledgehammer.

The story of Ruf Automobile GmbH begins in 1939, when founder Alois Ruf Senior started Auto Ruf. Over the following years he built up a relationship with Volkswagen and offered its VW customers attention to detail. In 1955, Ruf developed a full-sized passenger bus, and then went on to build up a bus manufacturing company. In 1958, Ruf diversified into Fiats and, in 1963, he added BMW to his list of specialist cars. With his son taking a keen interest, it was inevitable that when, in 1974, Ruf Senior died, Alois Ruf Junior would take over the company, concentrating on the Porsche brand with which Auto Ruf had been involved since 1963.

The first Ruf-enhanced Porsche was introduced in 1977. The car featured a 3.3-litre turbo-charged engine which offered vastly improved performance over Porsche's current 3.0-litre Turbo. This was followed in 1978 by a 217bhp, 3.2-litre, normally-aspirated 911 engine, based on Porsche's standard 3.0-litre unit. In 1981, in response to customer requests, Ruf introduced a five-speed gearbox to replace Porsche's own four-speed gearbox. In 1983, Ruf produced what it called its first "work of art", the Ruf BTR (Group B Turbo Ruf), a 3.4-litre, 374bhp,

CTR Yellow Bird: on its way into the record books at Nürburgring in 1987.

Group C Turbo Ruf (CTR) Yellow Bird.

turbo-charged 911. This 911 was a bare chassis construction, and represented a complete package of engine, transmission, chassis, and brakes.

In 1985, Ruf developed a 17 inch wheel fitted with Dunlop's newly-developed Denloc System tyres (a high-performance safety tyre originally intended for use on Porsche's 200mph 959). The Denloc system prevented the tyre from leaving the rim when deflated, and also allowed the car to be driven on the flat tyre. Ironically, Porsche did not use the Dunlop tyre, but chose instead to use the Bridgestone RE71 as original equipment. Ruf, however, used the Dunlop Denloc Sport D40 to great effect on its 200mph plus CTR.

In 1987 Alois Ruf Junior brought out the next generation of Ruf-enhanced 911s. Here was a 911 that benefited from every minute development detail and was not compromised by conservative thinking.

Ruf named this the CTR, Group C Turbo Ruf, paying tribute to the Porsche 956 and 962 Group C sports prototype race cars of the eighties. 'Yellow Bird' was a nickname given to the car in recognition of its colour.

Following on from the BTR, the CTR was also a bare chassis build. Although Ruf used its own chassis numbers, the original CTR (registration no. MN P 911) was taken from an 'H' programme Porsche chassis, Ruf choosing to opt for the narrow-bodied Carrera as opposed to the wide-bodied Turbo.

A lightweight 911 coupé with a high-technology, twin-turbo engine, it produced 496bhp and recorded a top speed of an incredible 342km (214mph) on the Nardo Racetrack in Italy. Engine capacity was increased from 3164cc to 3367cc by retaining the 74.4mm Carrera stroke, but the bore was increased from 95mm to 98mm. Adding twin KKK (Kühnle, Kopp & Kausch) turbocharger units boosted the power to 496bhp at 5950rpm. This gave an output of 139.3bhp/litre compared to the standard Carrera's output of 73bhp/litre.

Porsche actually managed to get almost 20bhp more per litre from its 959 930 Turbo-based engine than Ruf did with its CTR, but the latter was lighter and less comfortable. Using lightweight materials, such as aluminium, for the doors and bonnet, the body alone weighed 200kg less than the standard Carrera body. Weighing in at 1150kg (2535lb) the power to weight ratio was 407.8bhp/ton. The 959S, the lightweight version, weighed in at 1566kg (3452lb) and had a substantially lower power to weight ratio of 287.3bhp/ton.

Maintaining the 40/60 front to rear weight distribution, the CTR had excellent traction and power delivery to the rear drive wheels. The 17 inch wheels allowed massive 330mm diameter Brembo cross-drilled brake discs to be used. Compared to the 959, the CTR brake disc diameter was considerably larger.

Substantially stripped of all its extra weight, the original CTR was very basic in its final form. Standard Carrera body, fibreglass bumpers, 6-point roll cage, Carrera/Ruf twin-turbo engine, twin intercoolers, uprated Bosch Motronic electronic fuel injection

The sum of the Yellow Bird's parts make up something rather more than just a fast Porsche 911.

Brembo cross-drilled discs and Dunlop Denlok tyres.

In the right hands, power slide oversteer is made to look easy in the Yellow Bird.

MN P911 at Nürburgring.

CTR's 3.4-litre, twin-turbo, flat-six Carrera-derived engine pumps out a staggering 496bhp.

Even under extreme cornering, body roll on the CTR is minimal.

The CTR Yellow Bird in good company - easily capable of out-gunning Ferrari's Testarossa, Lamborghini's Countach and Porsche's 959.

and ignition system, Ruf-developed 5-speed gearbox, uprated suspension, Bilstein dampers, Ruf lightweight alloy wheels (front 8x17 DL with 215/45 VR 17 tyres, rear 10x17 DL with 255/40 VR 17 tyres), driver's seat, full harness seat belts, and not a lot else. The fuel capacity was increased from 85 to 105 litres, adding 72kg to the weight of the car when full.

The body shape of the Carrera was maintained, including the original rear aerodynamic spoiler. Lightweight bumpers replaced the original impact bumpers, the door mirror was integral to the quarter-light and above each rear wheel, set in the flared arches, were two air-intake ducts with direct air feed to the throttle bodies (on top of the engine) and twin turbo intercoolers (each side of the engine). The Fuchs alloys were also replaced with Ruf, five-spoke design, 17 inch wheels, and twin exhaust pipes made up the rear of the otherwise standard Carrera look.

Ruf data states, 0 to 60mph in 4.1 seconds, 0 to 125mph in 11.4 seconds, and a top speed of 339kph (214mph). Here was a car that in its day, quite easily out-performed a Ferrari F40, and showed the world what a Porsche 911 could really do if pushed. Ruf decided to use the standard Carrera body instead of the more flamboyant Turbo body because of weight considerations, despite the direct head-to-head with Porsche's own 930 Turbo.

Officially, Ruf built 29 CTRs using original factory-supplied Carrera chassis. It also converted a number of existing customer Carreras to CTR specification. These modified cars, unlike the original 29, still have the official Porsche chassis numbers.

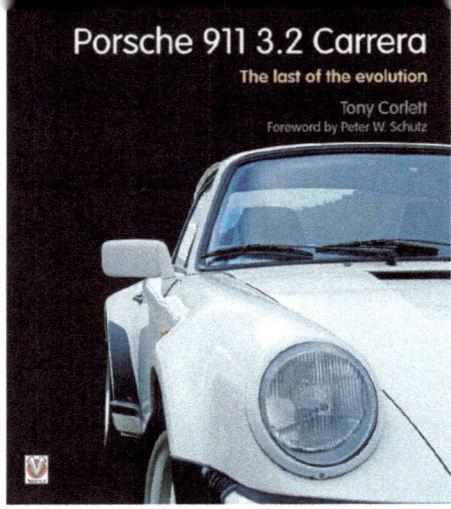

Chapter 27

Porsche vs Ferrari

Carrera vs 328

Both cars come from an era when traditional design features mattered. One comes with passion, however, the other with brute force; one was born from the heart, the other was born from the head. Porsche showed the way in the great 'mid-range' battle by introducing a 3.2-litre engine first, but Ferrari, not to be out-gunned in the 'affordable' supercar market, soon uprated its 3.0-litre car to 3.2 litres.

Whereas the Ferrari is low, traditionally swept and sleek, the Porsche is more upright and bullish. The Ferrari sweeps by, barely disturbing the surrounding air as it goes; the Porsche takes a more aggressive approach, confronting the air and forcing it apart with a mighty lunge. Where the Ferrari slaps you; the Porsche punches you.

So how do these two great cars stack up against one another? Both come with 3.2-litre power plants and both have fuel injection. Both cars carry the name of the company founder, Ferdinand Porsche and Enzo Ferrari, who approved production of these cars whilst still overseeing their respective factories. That's where the similarities end, though, as the cars are so distinctly different that it's hard to go from one to the other without taking stock.

The layout of the two cars is radically different: one is a mid-engined, strictly two-seater arrow; the other a rear-engined, 2+2 seater cannonball. However, as an art critic might compare the brush strokes of Picasso with those of Dali, so we can compare the automotive differences in such a way as to show that these two cars are exceptional in their own right.

One key detail separates the two, however, a small badge of distinction which places the 328 in the realms of 'designer' package. The Ferrari was born from the Pininfarina pen, whereas the Carrera evolved from the original Ferdinand Alexander 'Butzi' Porsche 901 design. This is significant if you are to assess the design qualities of both cars.

Interestingly, both were followed by arguably lesser cars, not in respect of their qualities, but rather in design evolutions. The Carrera was followed by the rather 'stocky' 964, an altogether different 911, and the 328 by the rather 'hostile' 348, also an altogether different car.

Before we consider the heart of each car, we can tell a lot about the engineers who designed them just by opening or closing the doors. The Ferrari immediately gives the impression of having to take care when opening the door, such is the daintiness of the handle, whereas closing the Porsche doors requires some effort. Then there's the sound of the doors, the instantly recognisable, deep-throat clunk of the Porsche door which releases as if ready for military duty, and the lazy, almost limp action of the Ferrari door which shows little inclination of opening, let alone allowing you to get in. The Porsche wants you to grab it firmly and deal with it, the Ferrari seems more languid. It's all about design versus practicality, with Porsche opting for the latter, of course, though with such high engineering quality, you can't fail to be

It's been argued that Ferrari launched its 3.2-litre engined 328 as a direct response to Porsche's 3.2 Carrera.

impressed. The Ferrari's designer door handles are soon forgotten, whereas operation of the Porsche door brings a smile every time.

The steeply-raked windscreen and steering wheel on the Carrera, together with the hugging leather seats promote a feeling of total confidence in the car. The long and sloping screen on the 328, on the other hand, complements the oppositely-raked steering wheel to great effect, providing a greatly lower roof-line and far sleeker lines from nose to tail. However, the Ferrari is not immediately comfortable, and does not promote the same level of confidence as the 911. It could be said that Ferrari designed its cars and then, almost as an afterthought, thought about where the driver would sit. How true that seems when considering the driving position of the 328. The Carrera pitches you upright, and lets you see far more of the overall car. The 328 lays you back and leaves you with very little idea of where the corners of the car are. The Carrera's steering wheel is right where it should be, ergonomically, and the layout will suit most drivers. The Ferrari's steering wheel stretches away from the driver, and the driving position is much less comfortable.

The interiors of both cars are impeccable. The Carrera came with the option of leather or part-leather, the 328 only came in leather but, compared to the Carrera, there is a suppleness not present in the German car. Once again, there is a design versus practicality debate, with the robust 911 winning hands down. The Ferrari seems much more delicate, to the extent that a stray fingernail might scratch or a sturdy shoe may cause irreparable damage to the tender finish.

The 328 has a cluster of instruments in a binnacle that sits high above the almost flat dashboard. The Carrera, on the other hand, has a wide instrument cluster, dominated by the tachometer, incorporated within the fascia.

There is one item that sets the Ferrari way out ahead, and that is the standard fitment steering wheel. I say standard fitment because Porsche offered two alternatives, both large diameter. The typical brushed aluminium triple-spoke, leather-rimmed steering wheel fitted to the 328 is sheer poetry in motion and lovely to use.

The Carrera is slightly longer, considerably higher, but lighter than the 328.

Frontal styling is also very different.

The smooth lines of the 328 vs the bullish stance of the Carrera.

The seats in both cars are very good and offer great support. The Carrera has the ability to comfortably seat taller drivers, and the seats can recline fully. The 328 is strictly a two-seater cockpit, whereas the Carrera can arguably be called a four-seater, the rear seats offering space for children or small adults. When not used as seats, the rears fold flat to provide a very useful luggage shelf. From a cockpit practicality point of view, the Carrera is way ahead in the battle, but this is to be expected given that the Ferrari engineers put the engine where the rear seats would normally be; the Porsche engine hangs out the back, allowing for considerably more cockpit space. The Ferrari is a mid-engine layout, born from the 206 Dino in the nineteen-sixties, and the Porsche is a rear-engine layout, born from the 356 in the nineteen-fifties. Both manufacturers were pioneers in mid- and rear-engine design, respectively, and both have a thoroughbred background.

Lifting the engine covers on both cars reveals ... well ... not a lot really, as the engines are largely concealed on both cars. The Carrera engine is dominated by the cooling fan, and the 328 by the injection box. The large engine cover on the 328 also spans a reasonable boot space, behind the engine. At the front of both cars is what might be referred to as a boot, housing the spare wheel, the 328 holding a good deal less than the Carrera in bulk. To be fair, the Carrera boot is not a bad size and will hold a remarkable amount of luggage.

Technically, both 3.2-litre units produce solid power, the water-cooled 'V' (33° 30') configuration, eight-cylinder 328 producing some 50bhp more than the air-cooled 'Boxer' or 'Flat' (180°) six-cylinder Carrera. Official factory figures show the 328 producing 270bhp at 7700rpm, whereas the Carrera produces 231bhp at 5900rpm, the Ferrari engine able to rev considerably higher. The Carrera also lags behind on torque, at 284Nm at 4800rpm compared to the 328 at 304Nm at 5500rpm. The bore and stroke of the 328 is 83mm x 73.6mm, and the Carrera is 95mm x 74.4mm, cylinder displacement being 3185 cm^3 for the 328 and 3164 cm^3 for the Carrera.

The 328 GTS Variant (1272kg), is heavier than the Carrera (1210kg), a difference of 62kg, effectively the extra weight of a passenger. This shows

Comparing the Carrera's 231bhp flat six with the 328's 270bhp V8 will not tell the whole story.

up in the standing 0 to 60mph times, the Carrera being quicker at just 6.1 seconds whereas the 328 records 6.4 seconds. Top speeds are quoted as 163.4mph for the 328 and 152mph for the Carrera.

Both cars are driven via the rear wheels, the 328 from a transversely-mounted engine, its gearbox below and behind the engine, whereas the Carrera is driven from a longitudinally-mounted engine, its gearbox ahead and in-line with the engine. Both have five forward gears plus reverse, driven through single plate dry clutches.

The Carrera is slightly longer than the Ferrari (4291mm compared to 4255mm) but the 328 is considerably lower (1128mm compared to the Carrera at 1320mm). The 328 also has a longer wheelbase (2350mm compared to the Carrera at 2272mm) though the Porsche has a smaller turning circle (10.95m compared to 12m).

At 1730mm, the 328 is wider than the standard-bodied Carrera, but narrower than the Supersport or Turbo-bodied versions. Ferrari never offered a 'sport' option for the 328.

In conclusion, both cars have their own unique qualities, and benefit from design and engineering supremacy to suit their own needs. They are exceptional cars, and very capable of producing stunning performance. Does it matter that the Carrera has more room in the cockpit, or that the 328 has a tenderly-crafted soft leather finish? Well, yes actually, these are important to the overall feel of the cars, and preclude us from ever trying to say that one is better than the other.

Porsche sold over seventy-five thousand Carreras, whereas Ferrari sold almost two thousand 328s, and in a way this is the only real comparison that can be made. The Carrera was virtually a mass-produced supercar, whereas those elite 328 owners could rightly claim exclusivity.

These days, you're far more likely to find high mileage Carreras than you are 328s. In fact, the galvanised Carrera is of such sturdy construction that it would well outlast the 328 in a straight head-to-head longevity battle. However, run both down the High Street and see which one turns heads. The Carrera is a head-banger and announces its presence with some force; the 328, on the other hand, seems to generate a different, more considerate reaction.

The Carrera wasn't designed, it evolved, the 328 was designed by the world's greatest car stylist ... but remember, beauty is only skin deep.

The radically different design philosophies of Pininfarina and 'Butzi' Porsche.

The Carrera's rear engine layout and the 328's mid-engine layout can both claim a long ancestry.

Porsche produced over seventy-five thousand Carreras, whereas Ferrari produced under two thousand 328s.

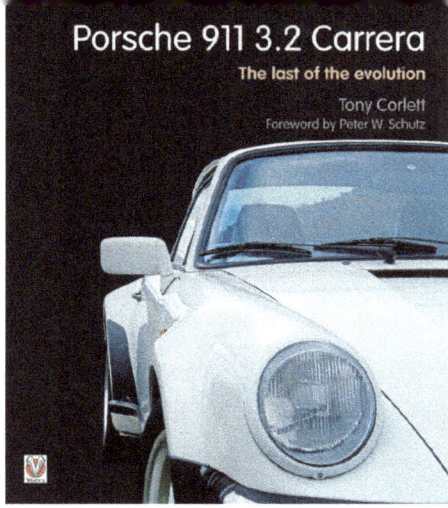

Chapter 28

Improving excellence: upgrading

There is a very strong argument which suggests that the Porsche engineers did their job so well that trying to improve upon their know-how and experience is going to be difficult. It must not be forgotten that Porsche builds reliability, longevity and economy into the overall package, so modifications to any factory settings will have a detrimental affect on one or more of these.

The Carrera was primarily designed for road use and, as such, has in-built limitations intended to create the perfect balance for day-to-day use. It was not developed as a race car and, although Porsche went some way toward this in producing an occasional track-day car in the Club Sport, the overall Carrera package is one of roadgoing excellence with little compromise.

The 3.2-litre engine is already near its expansion limits, so there's really nothing to be added here, except to say that simply upgrading one or two elements is not going to achieve much in terms of power, speed or handling. In fact, most upgrades will reduce the in-built Porsche excellence for sporting road use.

You should note that engine output needs to be as close to the 231bhp optimum as possible. Trying to overcome a lower power output with enhancements is never going to work.

Engine
Air filter - Fitting a cone filter or drilling holes in the airbox will only cause an increase in noise levels. The restriction in the standard intake is not the filter.
Exhaust - The standard exhaust works very well on a 3.2 Carrera engine. This engine likes back pressure, and changing to a sports back box, or even the early style or SSI type system, will not produce more horsepower without a complementary chip change. Cars with an SSI exhaust, sports 2-in 2-out muffler, and custom chip have been known to produce as much as 255hp at the flywheel. If you don't change the chip as well, you're likely to lose mid-range torque when changing to a sports exhaust. If you have a catalytic converter fitted, then changing to a pre-muffler will produce a little more hp than the catalytic converter alone. A complementary chip is required to realise maximum gains of 10-15hp.

Porsche Cup replica wheels are available with the Carrera offsets.

Split Rim BBS style wheels can be customised with Carrera offsets.

DME computer chip - You can upgrade the DME chip using a custom chip mapped on a dynometer. It would be difficult to gauge the effect of just changing a chip, though, as an extra 10hp in a 231hp car is less than most people would notice.

Engine management - A Motec system will control fuel and ignition requirements more precisely than a Motronic system, and can produce 260bhp to 270bhp if used with an SSI type exhaust and larger fuel injectors on a healthy engine.

Camshafts - There's not too much scope for performance camshafts in a 3.2 engine. Because of the shape of the pistons, there is limited valve to piston clearance. This means you cannot run something like an 'S' cam profile from the 2.4S or 2.7RS engines unless you invest in new pistons. A 3.2 engine with high compression race pistons and 'S' cams would be lovely. The 3.2 engine has enough displacement to avoid being peaky like the 2.4S, but an 'S' cam would give it a lovely 5000rpm kick. To get the maximum benefit you would then need to think about stronger rod bolts and racing valve springs with titanium retainers in order to run a little more rpm (perhaps a 7200rpm red line). In a standard 3.2 Carrera without piston modifications, the best camshafts seem to be the 964 M64 3.6-litre camshaft profile or equivalent. These will fatten the torque curve in the mid-range and allow the engine to rev a little more freely above 5000rpm.

Throttle bodies - This is the ultimate way to enhance the intake of the 3.2 engine. Six independent throttle bodies (ITBs) with six throttle butterflies allow a virtually unrestricted path to the inlet valves. They also sound wonderful. In the nineteen-seventies, the way to get maximum horsepower was via high butterfly slide valve MFI. These are great on a racing engine (like the 1974 RSR) but aren't practical for lower revs and road use. Independent throttle bodies together with a Motec, or similar, EMS control, is the most effective way to get 100bhp per litre without drawbacks.

A Carrera with independent throttle bodies, a Motec EMS, 964 camshafts and an SSI exhaust should make close to 280hp. Add in 'S' camshafts and racing pistons and the Carrera 3.2 engine is good for 300-320hp!

Engine capacity - It's possible to increase the capacity to 3.4 or 3.5 litres (with piston and crankshaft upgrades, using either 98mm or 100mm pistons). Going to 3.5 litres involves some crankcase machine work, so it is more difficult. The horsepower increase is basically proportional to the displacement increase. So 3.4 litres is probably only a 6-7 per cent increase. It's been shown, however, that lightweight racing pistons will produce a little more horsepower than the displacement increase alone would suggest. Combined with a camshaft change and SSI exhaust, the gains seem to be exponential. Porsche Special Works offered these conversions, so they're quite reliable. Helmuth Bott, for instance, drove a 3.5-litre 911 SC as his personal car.

Transmission - Type 915 vs Getrag G50. The G50 weighs about 40lb more than the 915, but has a more accurate shift. A good 915 may be nearly as good - in fact many Porsche fans prefer it - but there's always a little more risk of a missed gear change. There are 'short-shift' kits that create a more strongly sprung and 'gated' feel for the 915. There is also a completely gated shift to create a G50 feel.

Limited slip differential - Nice if you have one, but not worth the money if you don't. The reason is that the weight distribution of the 911 (60 per cent to the rear) means that, under power the rear squats very evenly coming out of corners, and there is very little chance of spinning the inside wheel. The only time you get inside wheel spin is in steeply off-camber corners, more so in the wet. If you have massive horsepower increases, then a plate-type or torque sensing LSD makes sense. 500bhp Turbos, for example, need such a differential.

Gearing - With a close ratio gear set installed, it will feel like you've added

30+bhp. An 'active' gear set will have a tall first gear, that is, one you actually use on the race track for slow corners rather than just for starting, and then closely stacked ratios thereafter (maybe not so practical for street use). Alternatively, you can lower the top gears, and have shorter 3rd, 4th and 5th gears. This will sacrifice some top speed, maybe only 10mph, but give a closely stacked 2nd, 3rd, 4th and 5th. Running a chip with the Club Sport rev limit of 6850rpm will go some way towards eliminating the pick-up in the gear spacing.

Clutch - The standard clutch works well unless you like drag racing starts. A racing clutch with a lightweight pressure plate and flywheel is a bit like an on/off switch, and makes street driving harder. Unless you need to replace the clutch, it should not be high on the list of priorities.

HANDLING

Alignment - Alignment settings involve a trade-off between corner grip and wear. Modern radial race tyres like a lot of camber - some as much as 5 degrees of negative camber. Porsche designed the Carrera to have some built-in understeer for safety, and the standard alignment settings are very conservative. They are fine for road use, but if you're performance-minded you'll want a little more negative camber. The more negative camber, however, the more the inside of your tyres will wear.

With a low ride height, you can almost get 2 degrees of negative camber in the front. The rear has more adjustment, achieving 3.5 degrees easily. More is not necessarily better, though, and most experts advise that you set the front camber first, and then set the rear at 0.5-1.0 degree more negative camber. A fast road setting, for example, would be 0.75 degrees negative at the front, and 1.25 degrees negative at the rear. This is about the most you will get at the front at standard ride heights.

To get more negative camber, you could fit adjustable camber plate top mounts to the front struts, lower the ride height, and use an adjustable strut brace to pull the shock towers together a little. Rear wheel toe-in should always be left at factory settings (likewise at the front, unless you want a very 'pointy' front end that responds very quickly to turn-in, in which case you can run zero toe at the front). Castor should be set to the maximum possible since more castor gives more negative camber as the wheels are turned.

Ride height - This depends on your preference for aesthetics and road clearance. Very low will adversely affect the front and rear geometry and, in particular, increase bump steer, requiring steering rack spacers. The tie-rods should be basically horizontal when the car is at rest. A lower height will lower the roll centres, which has a cornering benefit. Too low will mean the suspension operates outside its optimal arc of travel, though, and there will be adverse camber changes and the possibility of the dampers running out of travel. Adjustments are easily made on the front using the ride height adjustment screws, while small adjustments on the rear can be achieved using the eccentric bolts on the spring-plate. Bigger adjustments on the rear require re-indexing and removal of the rear torsion bars. Whenever ride height is changed, you'll need to re-align the car, as ride height affects the geometry.

Dampers - Your choice of damper will always involve a compromise between comfort and stiffness, in relation to road conditions. Most Carreras had Boge gas dampers fitted as standard. Porsche deemed them good enough and, provided they are in good working order, they work very well. For road use, these dampers provide a nice ride/handling balance. A stiffer damper would provide better body control and less weight transfer. The sportier dampers supplied by Bilstein for the Carrera come in two alternatives: Heavy Duty and Sport. Heavy Duty is slightly too hard when used with standard torsion bars, but worthwhile for track use. Sport is less hard, but provides a very stiff setting for everyday road use on standard torsion bars. If used in conjunction with larger diameter torsion bars, the Sport dampers are very good. A combination of Hard and Sport (front and rear, respectively) when upgrading to large diameter torsion bars is not uncommon in America. Bilstein also makes inserts to fit the Boge strut.

Torsion bars - These are effectively the springs on the 3.2 Carrera. Increasing the diameter of the torsion bar increases the spring rate. A traditionally-recommended fast road set up would be to install 26mm 911 Turbo torsion bars on the rear and leave the front as standard. This will help counter the understeer, but will have little effect on ride. To virtually eliminate body roll will require the use of larger diameter torsion bars (though some front/rear combinations can make the car too firm for road use). A good compromise would be a 22/29 front to rear setup. While this won't result in a move towards oversteer, it will have a noticeable understeer balance much like the factory car, it will mean very little weight transfer due to the roll stiffness. A 22/29 torsion bar platform is certainly a much stiffer setup than standard, but the ride remains quite tolerable for road use if the damping is unchanged.

Anti-roll bars - Changing these is a relatively inexpensive way of making your car corner with less roll. An adjustable bar offers the ability to increase or decrease roll stiffness by changing the leverage on the bar itself. Bigger is not necessarily better, however, as anti-roll bars have a detrimental affect on ride. A nice upgrade would be to add an adjustable rear anti-roll bar, of a slightly bigger diameter than stock - say a 22mm diameter. This small increase in rear roll stiffness goes some way towards dialling out the inherent understeer and, together with new shocks and a fast road alignment, might be a good starting point if you want to compete in more than just the occasional track day.

Steering arms - The upgrade to Turbo tie-rods is popular. The theory is that by using a tie-rod with monoball type joints and no rubber, you get more precise execution of your steering inputs. If, for example, you needed to replace your steering rack, then it might be a good time to do the tie-rods as well.

Strut brace - Under certain stresses the front strut towers may spread apart or compress together. Hard cornering, for example, has been shown to spread the towers apart. It is this spreading that the strut brace is designed to correct, as even a very small movement may translate into a relatively large camber change. Targas and Cabriolets seem to benefit more from a brace than Coupés, but the difference my be so marginal as to be difficult to detect.

Suspension bushes - Worn bushes allow excess and uncontrolled movement. Whenever analysing suspension changes, you must remember that the goal is to minimise geometry change so that the contact patch of the tyre is maximised.

Using new rubber bushes will provide good compliance and isolation from noise. For the ultimate precision, however, a monoball upgrade provides free movement but zero compliance and noise isolation, though these are more suited to race cars where they can be regularly inspected for wear. In everyday road use, dirt, road grime and grit can cause failures.

A further option is plastic or Teflon impregnated plastic. These have to be fitted very carefully, and regularly lubricated to avoid friction and squeaking. A more costly option is polybronze bushings. These have zero friction, are easy to fit and to lubricate without removal, and they provide precise location.

The key bushing in the 911 suspension system is the rear spring-plate. These are large donut-shaped bushings, vulcanised to the spring-plate, and can deform over time with the constant load they experience. They are key because the toe and camber for the rear wheels are set from the eccentric bolts in the spring-plate. Sloppy bushings here result in sloppy rear wheel control, and adverse toe changes, in particular, result in oversteer. The cheapest and most popular change here is to use a harder rubber bushing.

BRAKES

Although the standard brakes on a Carrera are really very good, one limitation is that they are designed to fit within 15-inch wheels. As a result, are very similar to the brakes fitted to the original 911, which had roughly half the horsepower of the Carrera, and weighed a lot less.

Fluid - To avoid brake fade, use fresh brake fluid (preferably with a high boiling point). While the Carrera brakes are very good for road use, on a track day they will experience much greater demands than on the road, and will, therefore, generate a lot more heat. Using a race-type fluid is a good first step towards preventing brake fade.

Cooling - Better cooling will help to prevent brake fade and will also help to prolong the lifespan of brake pads, callipers, seals, etc. The first step is to remove the dust shields from the back of the disc. The next step is to duct some air to the brakes. Fitting a kit with scoops that collect air from the

Later 'modern' wheels can also be fitted to Carreras.

air stream below the A-arm and duct it to the centre of the disc is a good start, and although they don't collect a huge amount of air, they will probably collect enough.

Hoses - A popular upgrade is to change the OE rubber hoses for braided stainless hoses as these don't expand under pressure.

Pads - A pad upgrade involves fitting pads that operate at a higher temperature. It is a compromise again, however, as high temperature pads will not work as well when cold, their coefficient of friction is lower when cold. They may have little bite when cold, may create lots of dust, may squeal, and may even accelerate disc wear. They will, however, work at temperatures as high as 700-800 Fahrenheit. The cold performance of a race pad is never quite as bad a some people will have you believe, and will be tolerable on the street if you are careful, aware of the limitations, and drive accordingly. Porsche used Pagid pads in all its factory race cars, and these are very highly regarded. The 'Blue' compound is acceptable for street and track, and the 'Orange' and 'Black' compounds are more race oriented.

Discs - There are two ways of improving the brake discs. The first is to use the 911 Turbo brakes (which are very good, and their origins go back to the 917), but these are expensive, and the callipers are difficult to come by. The Turbo discs are 32mm thick (front) and 28mm thick (rear), and offer a much greater heat sink capacity. Another option is to use the brakes from an early 944 Turbo or 964. The 28mm thick 944 Turbo front discs and the 4-piston callipers from either the 944 Turbo or the 964 can be adapted to fit on the front, provided the standard Carrera proportioning valve is removed. This will result in an acceptable bias when used with the standard rear brakes. You need to run a 16x7 front wheel with this set-up, as the diameter of the disc and thickness of the calliper will not fit within a 16x6 or a 15-inch wheel.

Master cylinders - In general terms, the standard 3.2 master cylinder is fine for upgrades up to and including the 944 Turbo brakes. However, once you go to 911 Turbo brakes then you need the bigger, 930 master cylinder to push enough fluid around.

Wheels and tyres

Although the Fuchs wheel is very strong and lightweight, the design is quite poor for brake cooling. Using 50 profile tyres on the 7 or 8x15 inch wheels gives a nice gearing reduction for better acceleration, but the 205/50x15 front tyre, is quite small for the Carrera.

For the 16 inch wheels, you have a couple of options. The first would be to stick with the standard wheel and tyre sizes, 205/55x16 at the front and 225/50x16 at the rear, and add 20mm spacers front and rear to fill out the wheelarches and provide a slightly wider track. The second would be to fit some 8x16 or 9x16 wheels to the rear, and move the 7x16 wheels to the front. You can run the standard tyre sizes on these rims, which will give you a nice increase in track, but this will also stretch out the tyres so they perform closer to their optimum.

You also have the option to go 'plus 1' on 16-inch rims by running 245/45x16 at the rear and 225/50x16 at the front. Clearance at the rear is no problem, but you have to be careful at the front. Even a 205/55 on a 7x16 can foul the wheelarch at the front, and a 225/50 will be even tighter. You may need to roll the lip of the fender and run some negative camber to avoid fouling. A strut brace is useful for pulling in a little more negative camber, and using a 225/45x16 on the front also helps as it's not such a tall tyre.

If you use a 9x16 rear wheel, it's better to run the plus 1 size tyre (245/45x16) as this rim is a little too wide for a 225 section tyre. Most of the extra offset is on the inside of the 9x16 wheel, so clearance is not a problem, though you should check that there's no rubbing on the oil lines, spring-plate bolts, and on the wheelarches. If you're inclined to play around with wheels and tyres, it's very useful to fit longer wheels studs with steel wheel nuts, and have a few 7mm spacers available. This way you can make adjustments until you find the right setting.

The easiest wheel upgrades involve fitting the Cup replicas, in Cup 1, 2 or 3 styles. These are made specifically for pre-964 911s with the correct offsets. The later cars, 964s and 993s, have a different offset. The wheels fitted to those later cars need very big spacers in order to work on a 911 Carrera. The replica wheels have two disadvantages, however, in that they're very heavy, and they're not very strong.

Other options that work are the three-piece, split-rim style. Because

911 Carrera

these can be built from different rim sections, the offsets can be customised. Another possibility is the one-piece, 17-inch wheels from Ruf.

Tyres - The biggest decision, in terms of the compromise involved, is whether to go for R-compound, often referred to as track day tyres, or with normal road tyres. R-compound tyres will be very lightly treaded, and will have a very soft compound and stiff sidewalls. They can wear out in as little as 2000-5000 miles of road driving, but may last longer than road tyres for pure track miles as they are not so prone to overheating. In damp conditions, sticky R-compound tyres will have more grip than road tyres, but in the wet they are prone to aquaplaning due to minimum tread and shallow tread depth.

Tyre pressure - Porsche recommends very high rear tyre pressures, which presumably are well suited to sustained high speed running on the autobahns. Most people recommend that rear pressures should be around 2-4psi higher than front pressures, with front pressures somewhere around the 29-31psi mark. There is no absolute right answer though.

You need to regularly check pressures and wear across the tyre. Alignment settings, particularly camber, will change wear patterns. You will tend to wear the insides of the tyres more quickly with lots of negative camber, for example. Track days will put much higher demands on your tyres. With higher speeds, heavy braking and acceleration, higher g-loads and more friction, the tyres generate lots of heat and, accordingly, pressures rise. You need to monitor this temperature-related pressure increase when at a track day. This will be around 6-10psi above cold pressures. The optimum hot pressure will vary from tyre to tyre but, for most road tyres, the ideal is around 36psi, and around 32psi for R-compounds.

Once you find the optimum pressures, you can start to measure inside, outside and centre temperatures with a pyrometer, as a more accurate way to fine tune pressures and camber settings, but there is neither time nor space to cover that here.

Interior

There are usually two main goals when upgrading the interior: reducing weight and improving safety.

Seats - Changing to shell-type race seats with sliders to allow simple forward and aft adjustment will net a weight saving of around 40kg. Shell-type race seats may not work so well with standard seat belts, and they make entry and exit from the car more difficult, but they do help to locate you securely in the seat so you don't have to grip the steering wheel so hard to stop sliding around.

If you add proper harnesses, it's a good idea to add a roll bar or cage, as you can be more vulnerable in a roll-over situation with harnesses and a shell-type seat. The thing to keep in mind is that your safety depends on many aspects of the car's design and set-up. Once you start changing one area, you need to consider its effect on other areas.

Seat belts - Although 4, 5 or 6 point harnesses hold you in place in your seat better than normal seat belts, particularly when used with a race seat, there are safety concerns surrounding their use. Harnesses have to be properly and securely mounted, either from a proper roll bar or from the existing factory seat belt mounts using a harness guide bar to control the angles. This is an area where professional advice will have a large impact on your safety.

Steering wheel - Many people change the standard wheel for something a little smaller, usually a 350mm wheel. This obscures the speedometer a little, but the feel of a slightly smaller wheel with a large leather rim is very nice.

Weight reduction - You could, of course, remove everything in the interior, other than the seat and steering wheel, in an effort to reduce weight. The Club Sport, for example, has had many of the interior luxuries removed, but you can go further. Comfort levels inevitably dictate to what extent you are going to save weight; that and the increase in noise levels which will result by removing all the sound deadening and absorbing materials, such as the carpets. Door panels can be replaced with aluminium skins, and the side and rear glass can be replaced with Perspex. The rather heavy impact-bumpers can either have their impact absorbers removed, or entirely replaced with lighter fibreglass alternatives. The same can be said for the front wings, doors, engine cover and hood/boot lid.

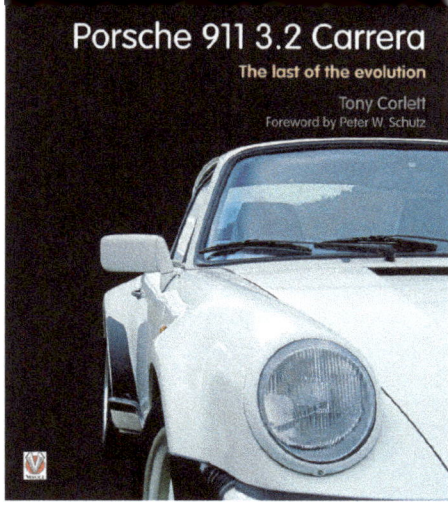

Chapter 29

Over the mountain

The Carrera has impeccable manners on fast twisty roads, and can be driven with confidence.

Set in the middle of the Irish Sea there is an oblong piece of land steeped in motorsport history: so much so that, today, it is known as the road racing capital of the world. Long since the dust of the very first motor race to be held in Great Britain has drifted into the annals of history, the sound of racing machines resonates around a circuit that has become a true legend in every sense of the word.

Still using some of the original 1905 motor racing circuit, the track has become a remarkable landmark that openly slaps the face of the conformist world in which we live. It stands out as a radical 'bad-boy' in an otherwise politically correct world and, in many ways, goes hand in hand with Porsche's 911. The TT course wraps speed with adversity, rolled into one dynamic package in which we can indulge. Is this the best Carrera road in the world ...?

The climax of this circuit is known as the 'mountain course' which winds itself up into a finale second to none. A finishing touch that leaves only the brave and the daring with a feeling of complete domination over one of the trickiest pieces of road in the world.

Mix the unorthodox with the unconventional and you get an explosive cocktail of adversity - step up the Porsche 911 Carrera and bring on a lap of the TT Course - welcome to chisel vs stone ... welcome to the Isle of Man ...

Twice a year, the entire TT Course is closed off for two of the world's greatest motorcycle road races, the Manx TT and the Manx Grand Prix. At all other times, the TT Course is a normal

911 Carrera

road with normal traffic and normal drivers. It is one of the main arteries of the island and provides circulation routes for everyday life. But beneath that lies the real animal, brought to life by those who know how, brought to life by those who can.

I want to take you over the mountain in a 911 Carrera.

Thrown in at the deep end really, the Ramsey Hairpin signals your first real dose of the Mountain Course. Just after the 24th Mile Marker, attack it hard, brake hard, too fast and you'll dig the nose in on the apex and get the tail out; too slow and it leaves you wanting. It turns sharp left, back on itself and climbs steeply through the apex. A stiffly set up Carrera will lift the inside wheel and traction is lost. Brake hard and square on the central white line, find second gear in good time, and turn the car in sharply, almost brutally: you need both hands here. Lay down the power carefully, too much and you'll swap ends, hit the throttle hard when the car is almost straight, the adverse camber will keep you pointing ahead and the climb up the hill will tame the horses.

It's gloomy at the hairpin, you're shrouded in trees and the side of a mountain stares darkly from beneath the shadows. Even in the warm sunshine, the hairpin can be damp and ready to catch out and punish the uninitiated. Punch a hole through the gloom, flat in second, up to the rev limiter and shove it well into third. Ignore the right sweep, keep it flat, it straightens slightly into another right, you might snatch fourth if you are cruising, brake hard and let the car run into the first of two right-hand turns, holding the throttle for the second tight right, stay in third, but watch the understeer on the way out.

You're travelling quickly now, climbing gently, lay the power on fully as you head out onto a short straight into a blind right, left sweep, nail the throttle in as it opens out up the hill past the waterworks. Fast in third through the left, right, left sweeps, lifting only to control the nose, and into the braking zone for the Gooseneck at the 25th Mile Marker.

The Gooseneck is tight and needs a big slow for careful negotiation. It's on a steep incline on a very tight right-hand bend which can be tempting to take too fast. Don't. Find second before you turn in, you will need both hands again here as you muscle the car in, taking care not to lose either end in the process. Too late on the brakes and you'll understeer wide into an awaiting bank, too early on the power and you'll spin.

You can plant the throttle almost immediately on the apex and sit and wait as the power comes back, gravity is tugging you back, all 60 per cent weight is squatting over the back wheels, and the 911 is shaking its head, surging forward onto the open sweeping sections of the Mountain Course.

Driving the Mountain Course fast is very much a matter of understanding the road and carrying the speed through bends. Keep it tidy, the smoother the better, don't cut the blind corners and on many occasions let adverse gravity, on the uphill sections, do the slowing down for you. You can save your brakes on the way up that way, you'll need them on the way down. A fast driver is not necessarily the guy who needs to brake everywhere, rather pace the car, roll off the throttle early.

The secret to acceleration in a 911 Carrera is to change up just before the rev limiter spoils the fun, and that's exactly how you snatch third, at around 6000rpm, out of the gooseneck as you head quickly into a blind crest left sweep. Hold it in third as the road keeps on sweeping left, into a short straight, left sweep, short straight. Stay in third for a tight right and hit the throttle hard for a long uphill run, sweep to the right, into a short straight, into fourth, over a blind crest and brake, back to third, for a tight left/right 's' curve at Guthrie's Memorial, the 26th Mile Marker.

Open out into a short uphill straight, blind left, short straight, flat in third through tricky right, into a left sweep, through a left bend onto the famous Mountain Mile, between the 27th and 28th Mile Markers, a long straight section in fourth and fifth. This is where the speed really begins to build up. It's all or nothing now, the Mountain Course is there for the taking, and where you were cautious with speed in the lower gears to begin with, you will stay on it now, catching fifth only for comfort and safety.

Into fourth through a long right-hand sweep, flat through a left sweep, the road keeps sweeping to the right as you climb up past the 28th Mile Marker. Stay flat up to the braking zone for a blind tight left curve at Mountain

On track or road, the secret to acceleration in a Carrera is to change up just before the rev limiter spoils the fun.

Hut, straight line the right kink and aim for the hut and brake hard. Accelerate through a second left sweep onto a long right/left/right combination, past the 29th Mile Marker. Stay on it in fourth, sweeping right into a short straight. The road flattens out a bit here as you head towards the summit of the mountain through a series of fast sweeps. You can stay in fourth here or choose fifth for comfort.

From here, there is a great view across the valley to the right, looking out for oncoming traffic to the Black Hut. This is important at this point, because of a very tricky right-hand turn, which can be taken fast in fourth using the whole road, otherwise it's brake time, and keeping the car on the left of the road is tricky on the adverse camber which has a tendency to pull you wide.

Assuming a clear road, you can accelerate down a short straight to the Black Hut very quickly indeed, flat in fourth, before easing the car out to the extreme right of the road and feathering off. No need to brake, Black Hut is a fast left-hand bend with good grip and visibility. Roll the car off the right kerb, brush the apex, flatten the throttle and let it run wide across the road to the right, before bringing it back to the left to set up for the first right-hand sweep into the Veranda, past the 30th Mile Marker.

Stay in fourth, ease off the throttle for a long sweeping blind right with four effective apexes and onto the fast Veranda straight in fourth. A long fast straight with a blind right sweep into a short straight. As you straighten out, the whole road comes into view and you can see across to the left through the next combination of bends. Once again, if there is no traffic, bring the car out smoothly as far as you can to the right turn, run the car to the apex and flatten the throttle for a short straight, let the nose drift out to the right, but no more than the middle of the road, you need to bring it back to the left smartly for a blind long right into the Bungalow. A very short straight into the Bungalow, used mostly for braking and finding third. The Bungalow is a deceptively slow corner.

Look across the series of Bungalow turns and up Hailwood Rise to Brandywell. Loads of braking on the right of the road, wash off more speed than you think, the Bungalow tightens back on itself and will catch you out if you're not careful. Stay in third, wait for the right moment, it is a long apex, before squeezing the throttle and letting the car have its head.

Suddenly you seem to have acres of road to play with, and you pay the price for the slow Bungalow. Onto Hailwood rise is a tricky off-camber right sweep which can only be taken flat on the wrong side of the road, but the car will still understeer, seemingly wanting to bury you into the banking on the left, but stay with it, feather off understeer for the timid, but you can plant the throttle as you head up the fast Hailwood Rise, past the 31st Mile Marker, flat into fourth and roll into fifth. Sweep right and feather off for the fast right into the tight left at Brandywell, brake hard, back to third, and keep the car tight.

Sweep left again and through a fast right, brake, stay in third for a combination of two left turns, at the 32nd Mile Marker, feather the power between the two and wait for the fast straight down to Windy Corner.

Look out across the valley and watch for traffic. At this point you can see for at least two miles and can assess the road ahead. This is important, it is here that you plan your approach to Windy Corner, another deceptively slow corner. The name of the corner gives you a clue, and yes, it can blow you all over the place up here.

Flat in third, and well into fourth before standing on the brakes, there is a slight hump and left sweep into the braking zone for Windy, but a great overtaking point under braking as you slip up the inside of the bend, the grip under braking is fantastic. Take as much of the left of the road as you can, bring it back into third and turn-in sharply, get the nose tucked in, the understeer will again drag you out. Stay off the power, it feels like an eternity, but eventually you will have the understeer under control and you can plant the power again for a long flat straight into fourth, flat left sweep and right sweep, brake for a long blind left, double apex, holding the car on the throttle between the two.

A short straight and fast right sweep, through the 33rd Mile Marker, tightening into a tricky braking zone for the tight left-hand curve at Kepel Gate. You will need to brake while turning in, it's quite easy to throw it all away here. Care is needed and some speed has to be forfeited in fourth through the right sweep. Stand on the brakes, select third, you can trail the brakes into Kepel but be careful, on a hot day the grip is not there and the car will slide around. Stay in third and hold it on the throttle along the short straight to Kate's Cottage. Keep it tidy in third through Kate's before hitting the throttle for the long fast downhill run to the Creg ny Baa.

Off the straight from Kate's and you can give it everything, shove the revs to the gunnels, you can hit the rev limiter very easily here, gravity is tugging you forward and your own blood pressure is rising. Then, sooner than perhaps you might like, stand on everything you have to slow down, you'll need it to get around the blind and very tight right-hand Creg ny Baa. Third is best here, albeit slow. It is at this turn that the brakes have to be in top condition, if you're inexperienced with the mountain and you've hammered them too hard on your way over, some fade might be apparent; be careful, you may like to dab the brakes with your left foot on the way down the hill.

Too brave and too late on the brakes and you'll go straight through the front doors of the Creg ny Baa hotel, too fast on turn-in and you'll go backwards through the establishment's car park. This is one of the slowest points on the course and, ironically, comes off one of the faster straights. It demands respect. Accelerate too quickly off the apex and you will understeer into the wall on the way out.

The final downhill run from the Creg ny Baa to Hillberry is very fast, narrow, downhill. A long straight, a blind right sweep, a short straight before hard braking for Brandish.

Nasty would be the best description of Brandish. Brake hard, bring it back into third, and don't underestimate the tightness, it's blind, but you can feather in the power on the apex before flattening the throttle for the last straight, a long run into the restricted areas. You can gun it all the way and let the speed wash off on the slight uphill run out of Hillberry and past the 36th Mile Marker.

You've come off the mountain. Just under twelve miles and it all happened in less than ten minutes. If you've driven it fast, your mouth will be dry and the adrenaline pumping - there really is nothing quite like a spirited trip over the mountain in a 911.

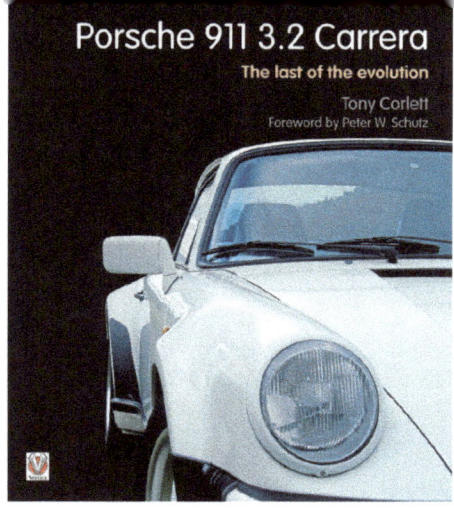

Chapter 30

Spirit of Carrera

So why is it that these cars exude such spirit? Perhaps it's the engineering quality, or perhaps it's the fact that no matter what, they give an immense sense of pleasure. Whether standing still or moving, the Carrera spirit never lifts, it's always there to grab you by the scruff of the neck and make you feel like something really special is going on.

It's generally known that the name Carrera was adopted by Porsche from the 'La Carrera Panamericana' road race that took place in Mexico between 1950 and 1954. Porsche won the 1953 event with a 550 Spyder, and it seems that, as a result, it took up the name and started using it on the competition-based cars, with road car derivatives carrying the Carrera name as a mark of sporting tradition. It is fitting, therefore, that Porsche chose to name the new 1984 911 a Carrera.

A spirit of competition is there, bred so deeply into the car that it's impossible not to feel the emotion that Porsche drew on in evolving its icon 911 into one of the greatest race-based road cars.

It is that same spirit which provokes the driver into challenging the very car that is seemingly infallible, by stepping over the thin line of 911 adversity. Pressed hard, the Carrera just keeps giving more and more until you instinctively know that you have wrung it by the neck and beaten it at its own game.

Like man and machine in unison, the spirit of Carrera lives on vividly, long after all is at rest and the machinery cold. The 911 3.2 Carrera really is a great car, in emotion and in engineering, a real place of combined business and pleasure. Long live the 911 Carrera!

1987 Targa.

1988 Coupé.

911 Carrera

1986 Cabriolet.

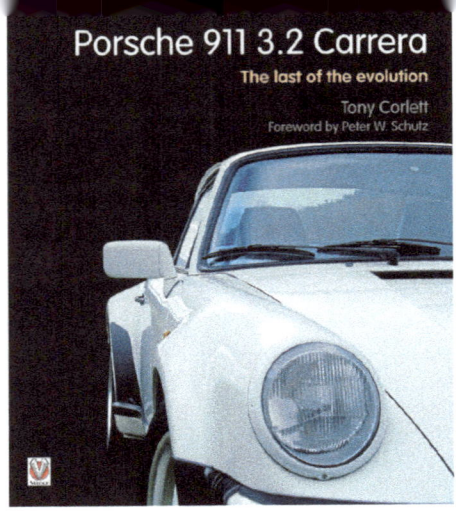

Chapter 31

Technical overview

1984 Carrera engine bay.

The 911 3.2 Carrera was manufactured from 1984 to 1989, and included Coupé, Targa, Cabriolet, and Turbo-Look (Supersport) body variations. This was the last of the 911 line to be designated as such by the factory, and manufactured under that number. Providing a nice blend of the classic and new, it was also the last car to carry the distinctive, and somewhat characterful, 'impact bumpers'.

With a flat-six 3164cc powerplant, the factory figures show a power output for the European specification of 231bhp, with 0 to 62.5mph (100kmh) coming up in 6.1 seconds, and a top speed of 152mph. For the two American specification engines, the factory figures show power outputs of 207 and 217bhp, with 0 to 60mph coming up in 6.3 and 6.1 seconds respectively, and top speeds of 146 and 149mph. With an unladen weight of 1210kg, the 3.2 Sport equiped Carrera has an excellent power to weight ratio: 191bhp/tonne for Europe; 171 and 179bhp/tonne for America. It can return anything up to 41mpg if driven with care.

The 3.2 Carrera stands as one of the Porsche fans' favourites. It has no electronic driving aids, no ABS, no power steering, and no traction control. In fact, it's driving in its purest form; a great combination of driver and car. Driven through the rear wheels only, maximum power comes at 6520rpm, with maximum torque at 4800rpm.

The engine is a 6-cylinder, 4-stroke, horizontally-opposed (flat or boxer) air-cooled unit, comprising a light alloy two-piece crankcase, forged steel crankshaft, forged steel con rods, forged light alloy pistons, light alloy separate cylinders (barrels), and light alloy cylinder heads. The valve arrangement is an overhead V-pattern, and consists of single intake and exhaust valves operated by a single, chain-driven, overhead, cast steel camshaft per bank.

The engine is air-cooled, the air being forced around the engine by a belt-driven, multi-blade fan, situated at the rear. The crankshaft fan ratio is 1:1.67, and the air flow rate is 1500 litres/second at 6000rpm.

Lubrication is via a dry sump with separate oil reservoir configuration. The oil, which also assists in engine cooling, is passed through a thermostatically-controlled cooler on the crankcase, within the fan air stream, and onto an oil cooler radiator situated at the front of the car, under the front right fender. From 1987 onwards, the front-mounted radiator was fan-assisted. Oil pressure at 5000rpm is 3.5 bar at 90 degrees C, and a pressure indicator gauge and lamp is located on the dashboard. Oil capacity is 13 litres and consumption is generally up to 1.5 litres/1000km.

The standard factory exhaust system consists of a single pipe system, with a junction outside of the heat exchanger, with primary and main silencers (mufflers). A catalytic converter in place of the primary silencer was standard fitment in America, and optional in Germany. The heat exchangers, which are attached to the main exhaust pipes, are located at the front of the engine, and direct warm air to the passenger cabin via electronic blowers and an automatic temperature control.

The fuel system is of the DME type (Digital Motor Electronics) and is the Bosch Motronic system. Fuel is pumped via an electric roller cell pump. Fuel tank Fuel tank capacity is 80 and 85 litres, for 1984 and post 1984 cars, of which 8 litres is the reserve.

The electrical system is a 12 volt system, fed from an outboard located battery. The ignition is electronic (breakerless), and the firing order is 1-6-2-4-3-5.

Earlier cars came with the 915 specification gearbox and cable-operated clutch, whereas cars from 1987 onwards had a G50 specification gearbox and hydraulically-operated clutch. Five forward gears and one reverse through single dry plate clutch, spiral bevel differential, rear double universal joint halfshaft axles. Final drive ratio is 3.875:1 for the 915 and 3.44:1 for the G50 gearboxes.

The front suspension set-up comprises independent wishbones turning on torsion bars fixed to vertical MacPherson struts. At the rear, the system comprises independent semi-trailing arms turning on torsion bars also fixed to vertical MacPherson struts. Anti-roll bars to the front and the rear.

With no springs, the car is weighted on the torsion bars and loaded on the dampers and, apart from increasing the diameter or stiffness of the torsion bars, the dampers provide the optimum adjustment for the car's handling.

The braking system is a servo assisted, hydraulic, dual circuit system, with internally ventilated discs on all four wheels.

The chassis is a rigid floorpan monocoque, making it extremely stiff.

The body design is a 2-door, 2+2 coupé, made from hot-dip galvanised sheet steel, with optional front and rear spoilers.

DIMENSIONS	
Length	4291mm
Width	1652mm (Sport Equipment)
	1775mm (Turbo-Look / Supersport Equipment)
Height	1320mm
Wheelbase	2272mm
TRACK VARIATION CAUSED BY VARIOUS WHEEL WIDTHS	
6in front wheels	1372mm
7in front wheels	1398mm
6in rear wheels	1354mm
7in rear wheels	1380mm
8in rear wheels	1405mm
9in rear wheels	1492mm
Ground clearance	120mm
Overhang angle	Front 15.5°
	Rear 17°
WEIGHTS (SPORT EQUIPPED CARS)	
Front curb weight	490kg
Rear curb weight	720kg
Total curb weight	1210kg

CAPACITIES	
Engine oil	13 litres
Fuel	85 litres
Brake fluid	0.2 litres
Screen fluid	8 litres
CARRERA COLOUR CODES : (OFFICIAL FACTORY CODES)	
1984	908, 027, 700, 32Z, 182, 956, 655, 20C, 661, 662, 811, 810 and 966
1985/86	908, 027, 700, 673, 536, 347, 492, 822, 33P, 33X, 33N, 539, 936, 20C and 961
1987/88	908, 700, 347, 80F, 10W, 499, 21M, 80K, 980, 35Y, 699, 40B, 697, 40D, 35V, 35U and 80D
1989	908, 700, 347, 80K, 60M, 548, 22C, 980, 697, 37B, 693, 22D, 81L, 550, 22E, 40L, 81K, 37B and 22E

Despite many owners believing that they have a Guards Red car, the 3.2 Carrera was never painted in Guards Red. The colour name is actually India Red (Code 027) later changed to Indian Red (Code 80K).

The wheels came in two designs. The aluminium alloy forged Fuchs wheels in 15 and 16 inch diameter and the light alloy pressure cast Teledial wheels in 15 inch diameter.

BODY TYPE	YEAR	CHASSIS NUMBER (ALL START WPO...)	ENGINE TYPE	GEARBOX TYPE
Coupé EUR	1984	ZZZ 91 ES10 0001 – 5000	930.20	915.67
	1985	ZZZ 91 FS10 0001 – 5000	930.20/26	915.72
	1986	ZZZ 91 GS10 0001 – 5000	930.20/26	915.72
	1987	ZZZ 91 HS10 0001 – 5000	930.20/26	G50
	1988	ZZZ 91 JS10 0001 – 5000	930.20/26	G50
	1989	ZZZ 91 KS10 0001 – 5000	930.20/26	G50
Club Sport EUR	1987	ZZZ 91 HS10 5000 – 6000	930.20/26	G50
	1988	ZZZ 91 JS10 5000 – 6000	930.20/26	G50
	1989	ZZZ 91 KS10 0001 – 5000	930.20/26	G50
Club Sport USA	1987	ABO 91 HS12 5000 – 6000	930.25	G50.01
	1988	ABO 91 JS12 5000 – 6000	930.25	G50.01
	1989	ABO 91 KS12 0001 – 5000	930.25	G50.01
Coupé JAP	1984	ZZZ 91 ES10 9500 - 10000	930.21	915.67
	1985	ZZZ 91 FS10 9500 - 10000	930.21	915.67
	1986	ZZZ 91 GS10 9500 - 10000	930.21	915.67
	1987	ZZZ 91 HS10 9500 - 10000	930.25	G50.01
	1988	ZZZ 91 JS10 9500 - 10000	930.25	G50.01
	1989	ZZZ 91 KS10 9500 - 10000	930.25	G50.01
Coupé USA	1984	ABO 91 ES12 0001 – 5000	930.21	915.67
	1985	ABO 91 FS12 0001 – 5000	930.21	915.67
	1986	ABO 91 GS12 0001 – 5000	930.21	915.67
	1987	ABO 91 HS12 0001 – 5000	930.25	G50.01
	1988	ABO 91 JS12 0001 – 5000	930.25	G50.01
	1989	ABO 91 KS12 0001 – 5000	930.25	G50.01
Targa EUR	1984	ZZZ 91 ES14 0001 – 5000	930.20	915.67
	1985	ZZZ 91 FS14 0001 – 5000	930.20/26	915.72
	1986	ZZZ 91 GS14 0001 – 5000	930.20/26	915.72

Body Type	Year	Chassis Number (all start WPO...)	Engine Type	Gearbox Type
Targa EUR	1987	ZZZ 91 HS14 0001 – 5000	930.20/26	G50
	1988	ZZ 91 JS14 0001 – 5000	930.20/26	G50
	1989	ZZZ 91 KS14 0001 – 5000	930.20/26	G50
Targa JAP	1984	ZZZ 91 ES14 9500 – 10000	930.21	915.67
	1985	ZZZ 91 FS14 9500 – 10000	930.21	915.72
	1986	ZZZ 91 GS14 9500 – 10000	930.21	915.72
	1987	ZZZ 91 HS14 9500 – 10000	930.25	G50.01
	1988	ZZZ 91 JS14 9500 – 10000	930.25	G50.01
	1989	ZZZ 91 KS14 9500 – 10000	930.25	G50.01
Targa USA	1984	EBO 91 ES16 0001 – 5000	930.21	915.67
	1985	EBO 91 FS16 0001 – 5000	930.21	915.72
	1986	EBO 91 GS16 0001 – 5000	930.21	915.72
	1987	EBO 91 HS16 0001 – 5000	930.25	G50.01
	1988	EBO 91 JS16 0001 – 5000	930.25	G50.01
	1989	EBO 91 KS16 0001 – 5000	930.25	G50.01
Cabriolet EUR	1984	ZZZ 91 ES15 0001 – 5000	930.20	915.67
	1985	ZZZ 91 FS15 0001 – 5000	930.20/26	915.72
	1986	ZZZ 91 GS15 0001 – 5000	930.20/26	915.72
	1987	ZZZ 91 HS15 0001 – 5000	930.20/26	G50.01
	1988	ZZZ 91 JS15 0001 – 5000	930.20/26	G50.01
	1989	ZZZ 91 KS15 0001 – 5000	930.20/26	G50.01
Cabriolet JAP	1984	ZZZ 91 ES15 9500 – 10000	930.21	915.67
	1985	ZZZ 91 FS15 9500 – 10000	930.21	915.72
	1986	ZZZ 91 GS15 9500 – 10000	930.21	915.72
	1987	ZZZ 91 HS15 9500 – 10000	930.25	G50.01
	1988	ZZZ 91 JS15 9500 – 10000	930.25	G50.01
	1989	ZZZ 91 KS15 9500 – 10000	930.25	G50.01
Cabriolet USA	1984	EBO 91 ES17 0001 – 5000	930.21	915.67
	1985	EBO 91 FS17 0001 – 5000	930.21	915.72
	1986	EBO 91 GS17 0001 – 5000	930.21	915.72
	1987	EBO 91 HS17 0001 – 5000	930.25	G50.01
	1988	EBO 91 JS17 0001 – 5000	930.25	G50.01
	1989	EBO 91 KS17 0001 – 5000	930.25	G50.01
Speedster EUR	1989	ZZZ 91 KS15 5000 – 6000	930.20/26	G50
Speedster USA	1989	EBO 91 KS17 5000 – 6000	930.25	G50.01

911 Carrera

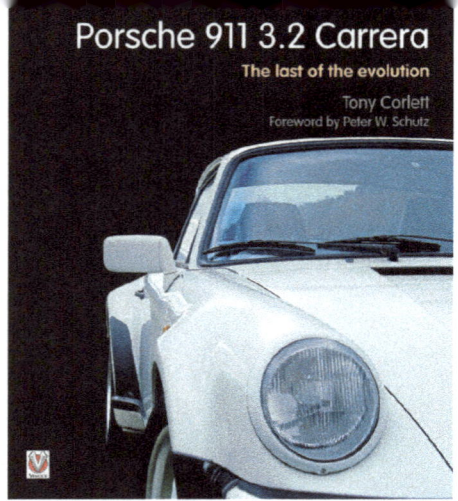

CHAPTER 32

TECHNICAL DATA

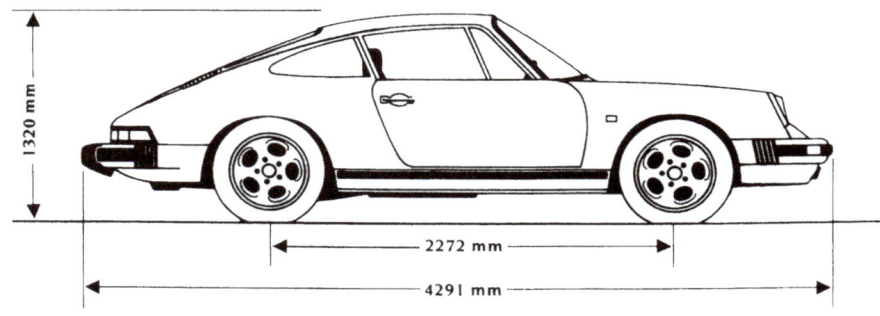

ENGINE				
Type	930/20 930/21 930/25 930/26	3164cc - 231 bhp - ROW 3164cc - 207 bhp – Catalyst - USA 3164cc - 217 bhp – Catalyst - USA 3164cc - 231 bhp - SW		1984 - 1989 1984 - 1986 1987 - 1989 1985 - 1989
Number of cylinders	6	Horizontally opposed (flat or Boxer)		
Bore	95mm	(3.74in)		
Stroke	74.4mm	(2.93in)		
Displacement	3164cc	(193.1 cu in)		
Compression ratio	10.3:1	9.5:1 (USA)		
Maximum power	231 bhp 207 bhp 217 bhp	170 kW 152 kW 160 kW	5900rpm 5900rpm 5900rpm	ROW USA USA
Maximum torque	210 ftlb 193 ftlb 195 ftlb	284 Nm 262 Nm 265 Nm	4800rpm 4800rpm 4800rpm	ROW USA USA
Maximum engine speed	6520 rpm			
Dry engine weight	219kg (483lbs)			
Crankcase	Two piece die-cast silicon aluminium alloy			
Crankshaft	Forged steel on 8 main bearings			
Connecting rods	Forged steel			
Pistons	Forged light alloy			

Cylinders	Light alloy Nicasil lined separate barrels			
Cylinder heads	Light alloy			
	Cross-flow hemispherical combustion chambers			
Camshaft	Cast steel			
	Single overhead per bank			
	Chain driven			
Valve arrangement	'V' pattern	1 intake	1 exhaust	
Valve guides	Brass	Press-fit		
Valve clearance	0.10mm	(intake and exhaust - cold)		
Cooling	Air-cooled			
Fan drive	Belt driven from crankshaft			
Crankshaft/fan ratio	1 to 1.67			
Air flow rate	1500 litres / second @ 6000rpm			
Lubrication	Dry sump lubrication with separate oil tank			
Oil cooling	Thermostatically controlled oil cooler on crankcase in fan stream plus front oil radiator under front right fender		1984 - 1989	
	Above plus fan to front radiator		1987 - 1989	
Oil filter	Full flow			
Oil pressure	3.5 bar minimum @ 5000rpm			
Oil temperature	90°C (190°F)			
Oil consumption	Up to 1.5 litres / 1000 kms			
Exhaust system	Single pipe system	Heat exchangers	Primary silencer muffler	Main silencer muffler
Catalytic converter	3-way catalyst in place of primary silencer/muffler with oxygen sensor		USA	930/21 and 25
Fuel system type	Injection	Bosch L-Jetronic with Digital Motor Electronics DME		
Fuel delivery	1 electric roller cell pump			
Battery voltage	12V			
Battery capacity	66amp/h			
Alternator output	90amp / 1260W			
Ignition	Electronic (breakerless) digital transistorised			
Spark plugs	Bosch WR 4 DPO			
Firing order	1 - 6 - 2 - 4 - 3 - 5			
SUSPENSION				
Front	Independent with wishbones and McPherson struts with torsion bars and anti-roll bars.			
Rear	Independent semi-trailing arms with torsion bars and anti-roll bar			
	Torsion bars	front/rear 18.8mm/24mm 18.8mm/25mm	1984/1985 1986/1989	
	Turbo-Look Turbo-Look	18.8mm/26mm 18.8mm/27mm	1984/1986 1987/1989	

	Anti-roll bars	front/rear 20mm/18mm 22mm/21mm	1984/1985 1986/1989	
	Turbo-Look	22mm/20mm	1984/1989	
Shock absorbers	Front and rear hydraulic double-acting gas pressure dampers			
Steering	Rack and pinion			
TRANSMISSION				
Type	915 G50	915-72 / 915-67 / 915-69 915-73 / 915-68 / 915-70 G50-00 / Europe and rest of world G50-01 / USA, Canada and Japan G50-02 / Switzerland	1984 - 1986 1984 - 1986 1987 - 1989 1987 - 1989 1987 - 1989	
Housing	Die-cast aluminium			
Gears	5 forward + 1 reverse			
Clutch	Single dry plate	Cable-operation Hydraulic-operation	1984 - 1986 1987 - 1989	
BODY				
Type	2 door 2 + 2 coupé All sheet steel Hot-dip galvanised Optional front and rear spoilers Optional wide-body	 Sport Turbo-Look	 1984 - 1989 1984 - 1989	
BRAKES				
Type	Hydraulic dual circuit – Servo-assisted			
Discs	Standard Turbo-Look	Ventilated discs all round Cross drilled discs		
Callipers	Standard Turbo-Look	Cast iron to front and rear Cast aluminium to front and rear		
WHEELS				
Type	Forged Fuchs light alloy Cast Teledial light alloy			
Size	6J x 15 7J x 15 8J x 15 6J x 16 7J x 16 8J x 16 9J x 16	Fuchs and Teledial Fuchs and Teledial Fuchs only Fuchs only Fuchs only Fuchs only Fuchs only	 Turbo-Look	 1986/1989
Tyres	Size	195 / 65 VR 15 and 215 / 60 VR 15 205 / 55 VR 16 and 225 / 50 VR 16 205 / 55 VR 16 and 245 / 45 VR 16	 Turbo-Look	
CAPACITIES				
Engine oil	13 litres			
Gearbox oil	3 litres			
Fuel tank	80 litres 85 litres	Including 8 reserve Including 8 reserve	1984 1985 - 1989	
Brake fluid	0.2 litres			

Screenwash	8 litres	
Intensive wash	0.6 litres	

DIMENSIONS

Wheelbase	2272mm	89.45in	
Track - front	1372mm 1398mm	54.02in 55.04in	6in wide rims 7in wide rims
Track - rear	1380mm 1405mm 1492mm	54.29in 55.34in 58.70in	7in wide rims 8in wide rims 9in wide rims
Length	4291mm	168.94in	
Width	1652mm 1775mm	65.04in 69.88in	Standard Turbo-Look
Height (unladen)	1320mm	51.97in	
Ground clearance	120mm	4.72in	
Turning circle	10.95m	35.93ft	
Overhang angle	Front Rear	15.5 deg 17 deg	

WEIGHTS (Sport equipped cars)

Front curb weight	490kg	1080lb
Rear curb weight	720kg	1558lb
Total curb weight	1210kg	2668lb
Max permitted	1530kg	3374lb
Max front axle load	680kg	1499lb
Max Rear axle load	940kg	2073lb
Max roof load	35kg	77lb

PERFORMANCE

Maximum speed	152mph (245kmh) 152mph (245kmh) 146mph (235kmh) 149mph (240kmh) 149mph (240kmh)	930/20 930/20 930/21 930/25 930/25	ROW ROW USA USA USA	 Club Sport Club Sport
Acceleration				
0-62.5mph	6.1 seconds	930/20	ROW	
0-60mph	6.3 seconds 6.1 seconds 5.1 seconds 5.6 seconds	930/21 930/25 930/20 930/25	USA USA ROW USA	 Club Sport Club Sport
Standing kilometre	26.1 seconds	930/20	ROW	
Standing ¼ mile	14.7 seconds 14.4 seconds	930/21 930/25	USA USA	
Fuel consumption	41.4mpg 31.4mpg 20.8 mpg	@ constant 56mph @ constant 75mph Urban cycle		

All technical data as published by Porsche A.G.

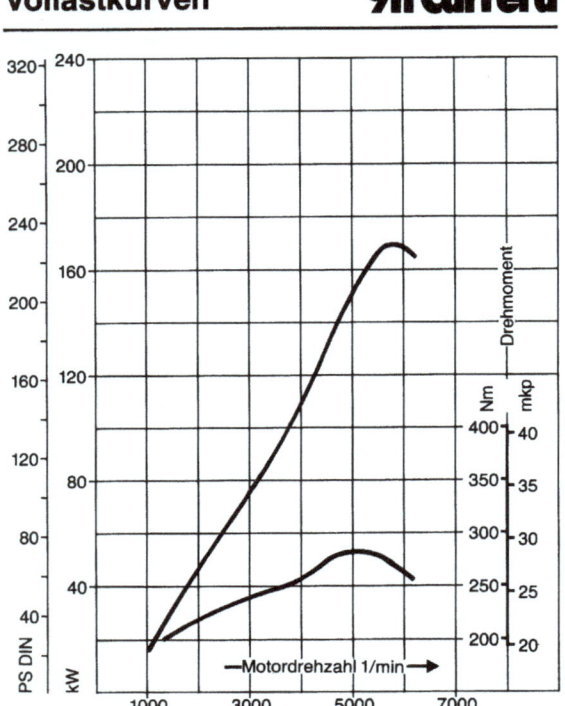
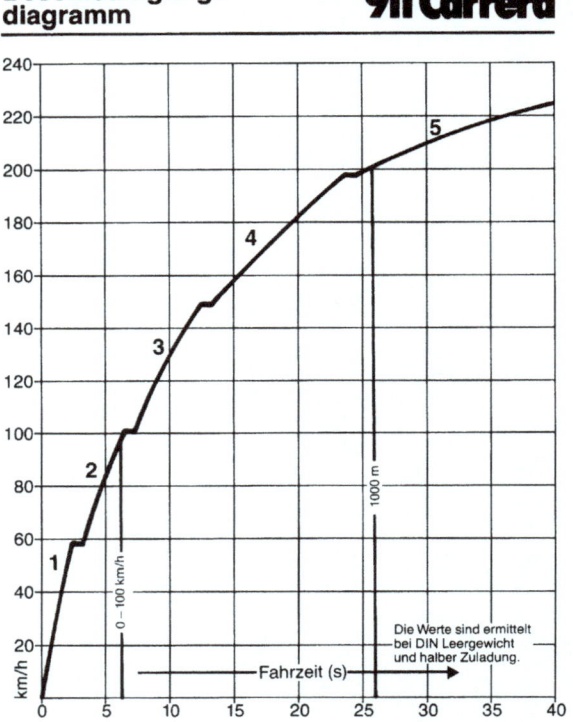
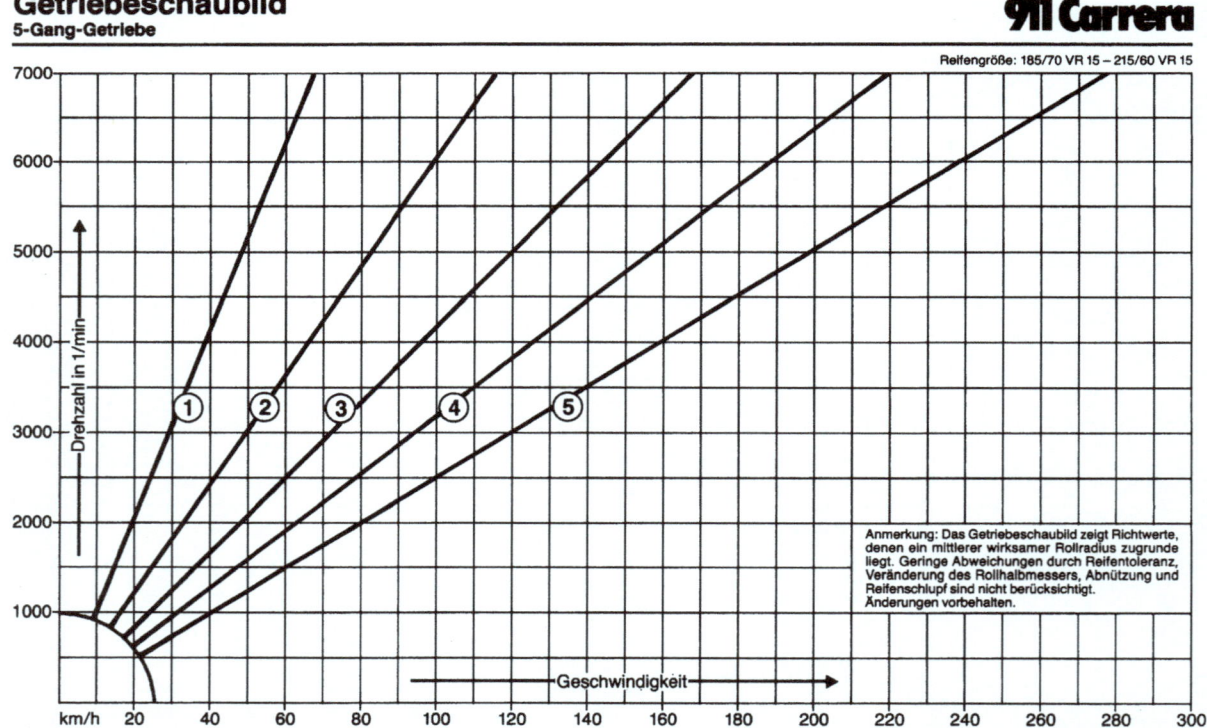

911 Carrera power charts.

Also from Veloce Publishing –

The Porsche 924 Carrera – Evolution to Excellence

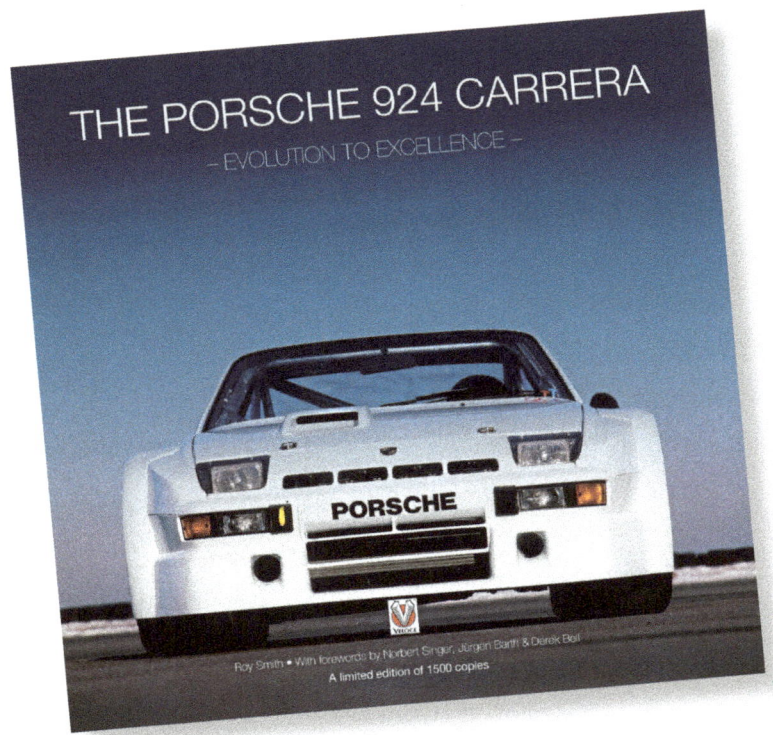

ISBN: 978-1-845846-45-9
Hardback • 25x25cm • 320 pages • 408 pictures

The 924 Carrera was a homologation model built to qualify the 924 model to race in Group 4. One of the great supercars of the 1980s, the 924 Carrera was considered by many to have better handling characteristics than Porsche's flagship 911. The book features interviews with many of those involved with the car at the time together with race stories, statistics, and a unique expose of component failures during racing.

For more information and price details see our website www.veloce.co.uk
• email info@veloce.co.uk, or telephone +44 (0)1305 260068

Porsche 928

This painstakingly-researched book looks at the birth of the 928, and then follows its progress around the world, taking in all of the variants in all major markets, as well as having a peak at its racing exploits. Illustrated with contemporary material throughout, it is the perfect guide to this eight-cylinder Porsche.

ISBN: 978-1-903706-30-5
Hardback • 25x25cm
• 208 pages • 431 pictures

Porsche 911SC – The Essential Companion

If you own, or are buying, a Porsche 911SC, this is a must-have book. Covering all aspects of ownership, including buying advice, maintenance, common problems, tuning, specifications, and much, much, more, this really is THE essential companion. Get the most from your 911!

ISBN: 978-1-845849-55-9
Paperback • 28x21cm
• 432 pages

For more info on Veloce titles, visit our website at www.veloce.co.uk • email: info@veloce.co.uk
• Tel: +44(0)1305 260068

Porsche 996 – The Essential Companion

Everything a 996 owner needs to know, plus a lot more, is contained within the covers of this book, in which every known model and version is described. With 1300 photos and extensive appendices, this fact-packed book is a must for any 996 owner. Get the most from your 996!

ISBN: 978-1-845849-54-2
Paperback • 28x21cm
• 656 pages • 1545 pictures

Porsche 997 – The Essential Companion

Describing every 997 model, Porsche 997 Porsche Excellence contains everything a 997 owner needs, plus a lot more. Transmissions, engines, and even engine management software for national variants is included. No matter where in the world, or what model of 997, it's covered in this book.

ISBN: 978-1-845846-20-6
Paperback • 28x21cm
• 656 pages • 1500 pictures

For more info on Veloce titles, visit our website at www.veloce.co.uk • email: info@veloce.co.uk
• Tel: +44(0)1305 260068

Also from Veloce Publishing ...

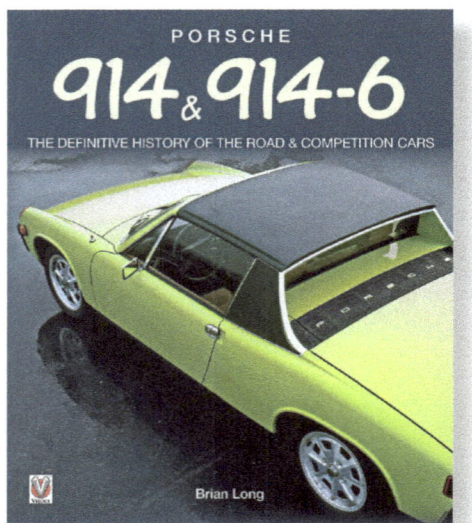

ISBN: 978-1-845844-92-9
eBook only

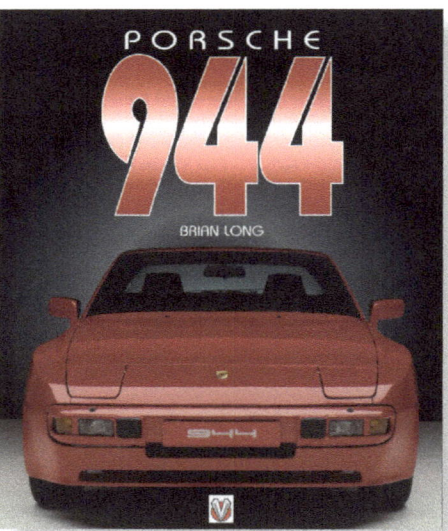

ISBN: 978-1-787111-35-6

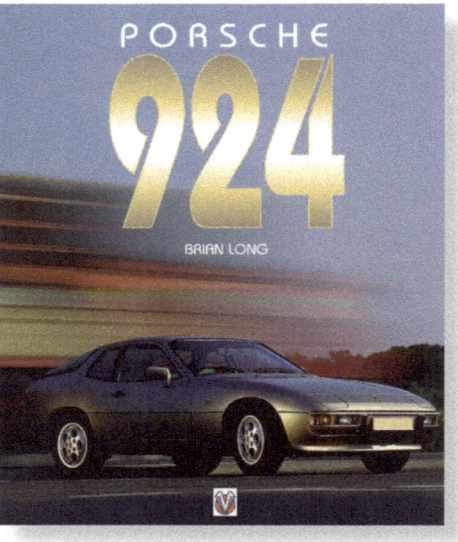

ISBN: 978-1-845844-72-1
eBook only

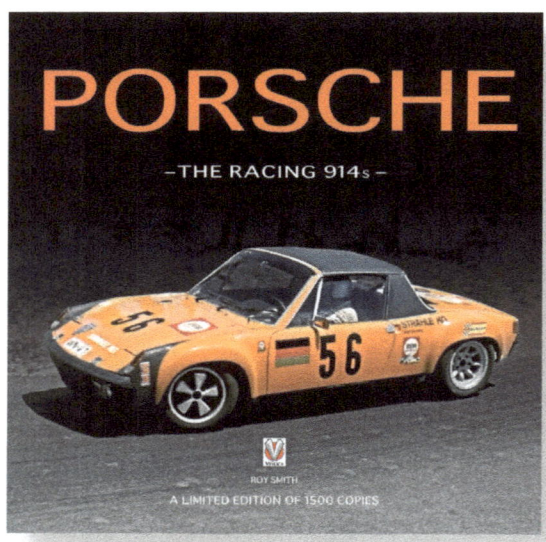

ISBN: 978-1-845848-59-0

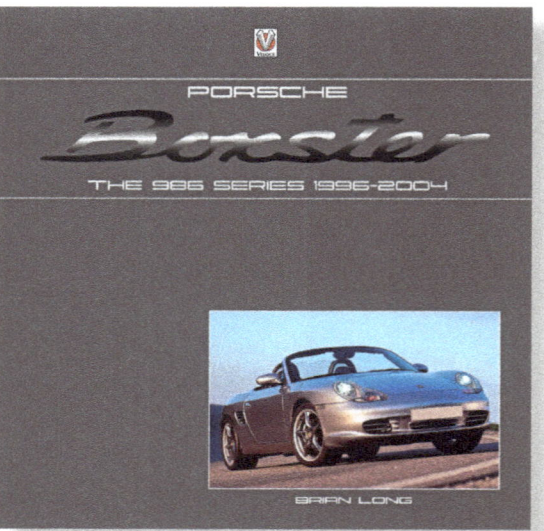

ISBN: 978-1-845848-04-0

For full details visit us on the web at www.veloce.co.uk or www.digital.veloce.co.uk

Porsche Racing Cars 1953-1975

Follows Porsche's year-by-year progress in top flight racing, and looks in detail at the pure competition cars that brought the German marque such immense success and worldwide acclaim on the tracks. This particular volume starts with the story of the giant-killing 550 spyders of 1953 vintage, and takes the reader through all the subsequent racing models.

ISBN: 978-1-904788-44-7
Hardback • 25x25cm • 272 pages
• 610 colour and b&w pictures

Porsche Racing Cars 1976-2005

Follows Porsche's year-by-year progress in top flight racing, and looks in detail at the pure competition cars which brought the German marque such immense success and worldwide acclaim on the tracks. This particular volume begins with the story of the pure racers of 1976 vintage, and takes the reader, car-by-car, through all of the subsequent racing models, including the glorious 956 and 962, up to 2005. An earlier volume covers the years up to and including 1975.

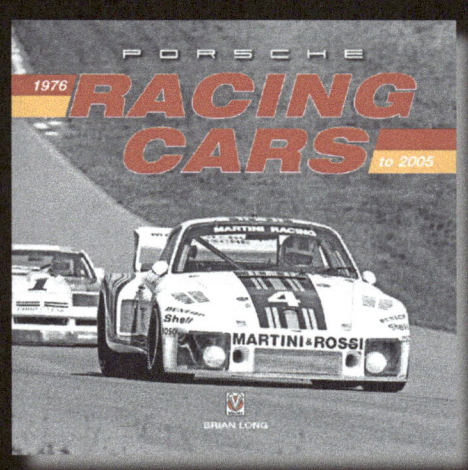

ISBN: 978-1-904788-45-4
Hardback • 25x25cm • 272 pages
• 629 colour and b&w pictures

For full details visit us on the web at www.veloce.co.uk/www.velocebooks.com
email info@veloce.co.uk, or telephone +44 (0)1305 260068 • prices subject to change • p&p extra

Porsche 993
The Essential Companion

If you own, or are buying, a Porsche 993, this is a must-have book. Covering all aspects of ownership, including buying advice, maintenance, common problems, tuning specifications, and much, much, more, this really is THE essential companion. Get the most from your 993.

ISBN: 978-1-845849-38-2
Paperback • 28x21cm • 640 pages • 1300 b&w pictures

For more information and price details see our website www.veloce.co.uk
email info@veloce.co.uk, or telephone +44 (0)1305 260068 • prices subject to change • p&p extra

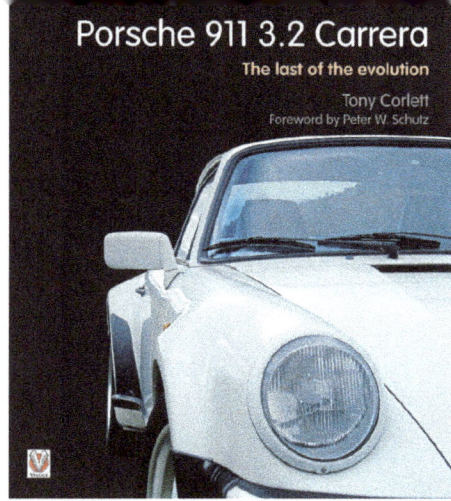

INDEX

Bauer 20
Bezner, Fritz 12
Bilstein 17, 38, 58, 68, 123, 133
Blaupunkt 66-69, 95
Boge 58, 133
Borg-Warner 13, 56
Bosch 11, 13, 38, 53, 55, 76, 110, 123, 147, 151
Bott, Helmuth Dr 6, 45, 46, 51, 75, 96, 118, 132
Branitzki, Heinz 75

Carrera Cabriolet 8, 11, 17, 20, 45, 46, 48, 61, 63, 66-68, 73, 74, 75, 134, 144, 147
Carrera Club Sport (CS) M637 7, 11, 17, 25, 28, 36-44, 46, 48, 54, 57, 63, 94, 95, 131, 133, 136, 146, 151
Carrera Coupé 7, 17-20, 36, 38, 40, 61, 63-67, 73-75, 119, 134, 144-146, 150
Carrera Silver Anniversary 7, 17, 95
Carrera Speedster M503 7, 11, 17, 28, 32, 45-52, 61, 63, 74, 94, 95, 147
Carrera Sport Equipment (SE) 7, 25, 32, 38, 63, 79, 100, 145
Carrera Standard/Non-Sport 7, 25
Carrera Supersport (SSE)/Turbo-Look (TL) 7, 11, 17, 20, 22, 24, 25, 28-35, 45, 46, 63, 64, 68, 69, 87, 128, 144, 145, 149-151
Carrera Targa 7, 10, 19, 20, 61, 63, 65-67, 73-75, 134, 144, 146, 147
Carrera Turbo-Look (TL)/Supersport (SSE) 7, 11, 17, 20, 22, 24, 25, 28-35, 45, 46, 63, 64, 68, 69, 87, 128, 144, 145, 149, 150, 151
Catalytic converter 11, 54, 65, 76, 131, 145, 149
Cup 59, 135

Duck-tail 24
Dunlop 119

Falk, Peter 115
Femppel, Kurt 75
Ferrari 123, 124-128
Frankfurt Motorshow 10, 20, 46
Fuchs 10, 33, 38, 59-60, 63, 87, 123, 135, 146, 150
Fuhrmann, Ernst 75

Galvanised 11, 20, 23, 66, 77, 79, 128, 145, 150
Gearbox 915 8, 10, 11, 13, 54, 56-67, 107, 132, 145-147, 150
Gearbox G50 8, 11, 13, 33, 36, 54, 56-57, 107, 132, 145-147, 150
Getrag 8, 13, 56, 107, 132

Halbach, Hans 75

Ickx, Jacky 115, 116
Impact bumpers 23, 81, 136
Isle of Man (TT Course) 137-140

Kahnau, Bernd 12
Karmann 89
Knoppen, Rudi 75, 96
Kussmaul, Roland 116

La Carrera Panamericana 25, 141

MacPherson 145, 149
Metge, Rene 115, 116
Motec 132
Motronic 13, 38, 53-55, 76, 123, 132, 145

Nardo 80, 119
Neckarsulm 75
Nikasil 53
Nürburgring 80

Pagid 135
PFM 3200 79
Porsche 917 31, 32, 135
Porsche 959 36, 116, 118, 119
Porsche 356 18-21, 45, 46, 51, 127
Porsche 901 10, 17, 18, 21, 22, 54, 124

Porsche 911 (930) Turbo 5, 10, 11, 13, 17, 21, 24, 25, 31-33, 53, 56, 64, 75, 89, 94, 118, 119, 123, 133-135
Porsche 911 RS 10, 31, 40, 53, 116
Porsche 911 SC 11, 13, 21, 24, 46, 53, 75, 94, 116, 132
Porsche 924 6, 56, 75, 76
Porsche 928 6, 75, 76
Porsche 944 6, 40, 56, 75, 76, 135
Porsche 953 4x4 115-117
Porsche 964 17, 59, 64, 124, 132, 135
Porsche Paris-Dakar 115-117
Porsche 'Butzi' A 18, 124
Porsche, Ferdinand 21, 75, 124
Porsche, Ferry 17, 75, 95

Recaro 89
Reutter 89
Ruf 118-123, 136

Schutz, Peter W 6, 20, 75, 96
SSI 131, 132
Stuttgart 25, 61, 77, 79, 94
Swedish Motorshow 20

Teledial 7, 63, 87, 146, 150
TT Course (Isle of Man) 131-140

Volkswagen 18, 21, 118

Weissach 76, 77, 79, 80, 96

Zuffenhausen 75-80

www.ingramcontent.com/pod-product-compliance
Lightning Source LLC
Chambersburg PA
CBHW040739300426
44111CB00026B/2986